The Safari Party

A Comedy

Tim Firth

A SAMUEL FRENCH ACTING EDITION

FOUNDED 1830

SAMUELFRENCH-LONDON.CO.UK
SAMUELFRENCH.COM

THE SAFARI PARTY

First presented at the Stephen Joseph Theatre in the Round, Scarborough, on 20th April 2002, transferring to open the new Hampstead Theatre, NW3, on 5th March 2003, with the following cast:

Daniel	Daniel Casey
Adam	Daniel Crowder
Esther	Christine Moore
Lol	John Branwell
Bridget	Amanda Abbington
Inga	Helen Ryan

Directed by Alan Ayckbourn
Décor by Michael Holt
Lighting by Kath Geraghty

Subsequently produced at the Library Theatre, Manchester on 15th April 2005 with the following cast:

Daniel	Drew Mulligan
Adam	David Partridge
Esther	Sue Wallace
Lol	Claude Close
Bridget	Lindsay Allen
Inga	Jenifer Armitage

Directed by Roger Haines
Décor by Judith Croft
Lighting by Nick Richings

CHARACTERS

Daniel, mid 20s
Adam, Daniel's brother, mid 20s
Lol, 50
Esther, Lol's wife, 50
Bridget, Lol's and Esther's daughter, 21
Inga, early 60s

SYNOPSIS OF SCENES

The action of the play takes place in three different households on a single evening

ACT I   THE HORS D'OEUVRES
          Daniel's and Adam's kitchen

ACT II   THE ENTRÉES
          Lol's and Esther's conservatory

ACT III   DESSERT
          Inga's outhouse

Time — the present

NOTE: INTERRUPTED SPEECHES

A speech usually follows the one before it BUT:

When one character starts speaking before the other has finished, the point of interruption is marked /.

e.g. **Bridget** If I hear the word "single" / in ——
　　　Esther Oh, for God's / sake ——

Other plays by Tim Firth published
by Samuel French Ltd

The End of the Food Chain
A Man of Letters
Neville's Island

To Jack, Joe and Georgia
Three wild animals of the county

ACT I
Hors d'Oeuvres

The kitchen of Daniel's and Adam's house

The room has two doors with corridors leading from them: one leads to the front door, the other back into various sculleries and pantries and other –ies. The kitchen is bare. The ripped lino floor (with gaffer tape over the rips) shows the ghosts of now-deceased furniture: a rectangle of totally different lino where the range was, four indentations and a relatively cleaner rectangle where a table once was. A fluorescent strip light hangs from the ceiling. One end has dropped a few inches

When the play begins, Daniel and Adam, two lads in their mid-twenties, stagger in from the indoor (i.e. the pantry) corridor at either end of a flatpack from MFI. Daniel has on a rugby shirt and looks as though he uses it on Saturday afternoons. Adam has on a skin-tight dance-branded top (with the words "2-Kinky" on it) and looks as though he uses it on Saturday nights. He is making the sound of a drum and bass track with his mouth

Daniel and Adam dump the flatpack on the floor and kneel by it

Adam OK. What are we gonna do first? Make the meal, or make the table?

The front doorbell sounds from the corridor

Daniel Who's that?
Adam The guests.
Daniel (*bouncing up*) Oh y'r kidding.
Adam I *told* y'.
Daniel Oh shit man, you are *kidding*.
Adam (*ripping the flatpack open*) I saw them coming up the Ridgeway. I told / y' ——
Daniel Oh for fff——
Adam It's OK. We've got time. (*He produces a sheet of instructions from the flatpack*) Grab these.
Daniel "Got time"? They'll be in the yard.
Adam (*handing the instructions sheet to Daniel*) Grab the / bloody ——
Daniel They'll be … (*He goes quiet; dead seriously*) I can't do this.

Adam Now then.

Daniel I've never put a bastard table up in my life.

Adam OK. First of all, stop swearing. This is not a couple who are gonna appreciate swearing.

Daniel (*quietly*) We can't make the table.

Adam It cost nine quid.

Daniel (*calm, calm*) They're in the yard.

Adam (*getting the parts of the table out of the flatpack*) It cost nine quid.

Daniel They're in the / yard.

Adam Nothing that cost nine quid can be hard. Now *take*. (*He pulls a large plastic see-through bag of screws and nails out of the flatpack*)

Daniel (*looking at the instructions*) Oh, it's eleven stages.

Adam What?

Daniel It's eleven stages, man. The instructions are eleven stages and look, even the bloody little stick-figure man's having trouble.

Adam Give it / here ——

Daniel Look at him.

Adam Just / give ——

Daniel Stage seven is him in a pub bitching about how hard the table is to put up.

Adam (*snatching the instructions from Daniel*) Dan. These are people who've bought a barn conversion. They are not going to give a gardening contract to a couple of lads who sit there going "shit bugger bloody".

Pause

(*Reading*) "Stage one. Ensure you have all fifty-eight screws and fittings."

The doorbell goes

Get me a hammer.

Adam starts to nail one pine leg into place using a screw and the other pine leg as a hammer

Daniel They're gonna think we're not here.

Adam You just — (*thrusting a table leg at Daniel*) get it started.

Daniel There was something else. Before they arrived, to do, that we … *The meal.*

Adam (*heading for the front door corridor*) What did I say their names were?

Daniel (*running in front of Adam*) They are coming round here to eat / a ——

Adam It's not a meal. It's just the hors d'oeuvres.

Daniel Oh well that's all right. Hoo. For a moment there I thought we were up shit creek.

Adam (*trying to get round Daniel*) There's loads left in the freezer from the funeral.

Daniel What?

Adam Dan, don't make this harder / than ——

Daniel Let me give you a report from the freezer, OK? Six pieces of rock hard cheddar cheese and an ice lolly. OK, now even on *Ready, Steady, Cook* ——

The doorbell rings

Let them ——

Adam Stop it.

Daniel — think we're out. Seriously.

Adam Move.

Daniel I mean what the hell — g ... (*He winces for the words*) Why are we having people round for a meal when you an' me don't eat anything that hasn't got a smiley fisherman on the box?

Adam Y'know, I thought that. When she asked, I was about to say, "We don't really do dinner parties." An' then I thought, "You've got a massive paddock, haven't you?" An' then I thought, "Maybe we *do* do dinner parties".

Ratt-tatt-tatitty-tat; knocking at the front door

Adam gives a little smile to seal the point, then disappears towards the front door

Daniel looks at the debris. He scuttles over and kneels by it. He gives the leg two hits

We hear the distant voice of Lol Voysey, off

Daniel panics, gives a little whine, bundles the table pieces up and scuttles off with them

Lol Voysey enters the room. Lol is fifty, in a light-coloured suit. His waistline is slightly colonial

Lol Oh-h the ... (*He looks round*) Ohh-hh. (*He laughs in approval*) Oh-hh-ho ho ho.

Adam enters

(*Turning and beaming at Adam*) D'you play golf, Adam?
Adam Sorry?
Lol It's Shell ...? What's it, y'r surname?
Adam Shellmedine.
Lol D'you play?
Adam Well, pitch and putt.
Lol Oh ho ho. (*Muttering*) We'll put *that* right. (*He holds his hand out for it to be shaken*) Lol, sorry. Lol Voysey.
Adam Lol.
Lol And this — is Bridget.

Bridget enters. She is a girl just turning twenty-one or so, in jeans and T-shirt

Bridget (*waving to Adam*) Hey. (*To Lol*) Guess what?
Esther (*off*) *Lol.*
Lol Oh, not again. Are y' serious?
Esther (*off*) *Lol.*

Lol exits down the front door corridor, cursing under his breath

Adam is left with Bridget

Adam Sorry, are you ... (*He points loosely to where Lol was*) ... ?
Bridget "I — am Bridget."
Adam (*gesturing in hope*) Daughter ... ?
Bridget Did y' like that? That little pause? Normally only used by magicians introducing their assistants. (*Producing a packet of cigarettes and a lighter*) Have y' got an ashtray?
Adam (*looking round*) Oh. Er ...
Bridget Don't worry. I'll go outside. Terrible habit.
Adam No no, s'fine. I'll, er ...(*He points where he's heading — the indoor corridor — and heads there*)
Bridget Have you been?

Adam hangs back. Bridget nods at his "2-Kinky" T-shirt

Adam Oh, yeah. Well not often. It's fifteen quid.
Bridget Cheap for a club.

Pause

Adam I'll, er … (*He points to the indoor corridor and follows the point again*)

Adam exits

Bridget lights up her cigarette, looking round. She exhales

Esther bustles in. She is fifty, well-built, in slightly glam damage-limitation evening dress. One leg is higher than the other due to a problem with her shoes — she has lost the heel from one of them

Esther Bridget. *Bridget, put that out.*
Bridget (*coolly, prepared for this*) They smoke.
Esther What?
Bridget Y'know there's alarms that don't react as fast as you.
Esther How d'you know they smoke?
Bridget Mum / just ——
Esther Look I don't want to get into an argument about this, but I remember what I thought when I first saw Pam and Arnold's daughter smoking, and that impression has never ——

Adam enters with the ashtray, a beanbag and a fold-out director's chair. He gives the ashtray to Bridget and puts the beanbag and chair down during the following

(*Seeing Adam*) Adam! Listen I hope you don't mind — it's not thrown your catering, bringing Bridget? Had you catered very specifically for five?
Adam (*after a slight pause*) Nn-n-no.

There is a loud clang, off

Daniel (*panicked; off*) Adam-m?
Esther We weren't expecting her back this week.
Bridget (*nodding in the direction of Daniel's shout*) Is he all right?

Lol strides in carrying the heel of Esther's shoe

Lol There we go. One snapped-off heel.
Esther (*sotto voce, through gritted teeth*) Dnnn't make a bggg fusss of ittt.
Adam Oh God, did it go down the grid? Y'didn't get any rat poison on y'r hand?

A slight frisson. Adam realizes there's a slight frisson

Esther (*suddenly smiling*) D'you get many rats?
Adam Well ... Y'know — (*he shrugs*) countryside. Y'r never more than ten
foot from a rat.

Lol and Esther smile. And slightly look around, as if to check

Lol Same as golf. Same as my line of work. Except there y' have to make
deals with them. Ha.

Pause

Esther Is this *all* left to you, then? To run?
Adam (*looking round*) "Sparkbrooke"? / Well ——
Esther Oh God! (*Putting her hand to her mouth*) Sorry. You just say
"Sparkbrooke" like it's ... ! (*Shaking her head*) "The Shellmedine brothers
of Sparkbrooke Farm". (*She beams*) *Pride and Prejudice.*

This causes a little pause

Lol Sorry to hear about y'r dad.

Another slightly awkward pause

Adam (*pointing to the lack of chairs*) Chairs.

Adam exits down the indoor corridor

Bridget Can I just say here and now, one word is banned from this evening.
Esther Bridget ——
Bridget If I hear the word "single" / in ——
Esther Oh for God's / sake ——
Bridget Either in connection with "Are you?" or "Bridget is", I will be down
that sodding drive ——
Lol *Bridget.*
Esther *Bridget.*
Bridget Because I am not "single". Am I?

There is a pause. This comment lands on the floor and glows

Esther I asked if the farm was his.
Bridget Yes, in such a way he could practically see the thought-bubble of
me being carried over the threshold.
Lol Oh, don't be so bloody / sensitive.

Esther He could not.

Adam enters with an old office swivel chair and another fold-out director's chair

Adam Sorry about the ... (*He gestures at the assortment of chairs*) Most of the furniture was just falling to pieces.
Esther Really?
Adam Dad wouldn't chuck anything. I mean the table that was in / here ——
Esther *God*, yeah.
Adam (*stopping dead*) Sorry?

There is a slight, awkward pause

Lol Don't worry, mate. She always starts cheering before the orchestra's finished.
Esther I was just agreeing, Lol. (*To Adam*) We've got a new table, you see. For our conservatory. I mean to be honest we built the whole conservatory round it.

Daniel enters with the bottle of wine and glasses (an odd selection, including a Coke-branded glass, one with a Silver Jubilee design, one with the Road Runner on it) carried tray-like on the table top which now has a large piece missing. He has a slightly bloodied bandage on his hand

Daniel (*sotto voce, slightly cowed*) OK. What's everyone having?
Lol *Oh, now would you look at that.*
Daniel (*stopping dead*) Sorry?
Lol See, no disrespect to Pam and Arnold, but they want a tray? They go off to John Lewis and pay sixty quid for a piece of hardboard with flowers painted on by some Korean copying bits of the National Trust catalogue, / and ——
Bridget (*sotto voce*) Dad.
Lol And what is a tray? *What* is a tray? Come on, what *is* a tray?

Daniel feels he's being pinned for an answer. He buckles. Everyone looks at him

(*Triumphantly, indicating the tabletop*) It's a piece of wood that you bloody carry things on.

Pause

Esther Have you read *Pride and Prejudice*?
Daniel (*suddenly panicked*) I didn't realize I had to. Has everyone else?
Esther No, we're in it! I'm saying, this is *Pride and Prejudice* we're sitting
   in here. A farmhouse kitchen. Two strapping young lads ...
Bridget This — is Bridget. Does y'r heating go up at all?

Daniel looks at Bridget

Adam This is Daniel.
Lol D'you play golf, Daniel?
Daniel Are y'cold?
Esther Bridget's used to the heat. She's been in Portugal.
Adam (*to Daniel*) D'you wanna get the fire? Is it in the log shed? (*He points
   down the front door corridor*) D'y wanna / see —— ?
Lol Also, if y've any orange juice or something?
Adam Oh right, d'you not ... ? You're not driving? No, obviously /
   you ——
Esther Lol doesn't. (*Breezily*) Drink.

*There's a slightly frosty pause. Adam has driven into a corner he now needs
to reverse out of sharpish*

Adam Actually I might've moved the fire in during lambing. (*To Daniel*)
   D'you wanna get the ... (*Nodding*) For Lol?

*During the following, Daniel exits down the front door corridor; Adam
exits down the indoor corridor*

Esther (*as they go*) See you just ... (*Waving her hand*) Phrases like "during
   lambing", you just drop them in, and for us ...

They've gone

   (*Turning on Bridget*) *What the bloody hell are you playing / at?*
Lol *What are you playing at?*
Esther Are you trying to make a point, here?
Lol It's cold in the country. This is how they live.
Esther Bridget?
Lol You're the first, can I just point out, to jump down my throat if I make
   a comment about how the French still crap in holes in the ground.
Bridget I say it because I'm cold. You say it because you hate the French.
Esther What?
Lol God. Y'know ——

Esther Your father doesn't hate the French.

Lol There's a word for people who turn into the bloody racism police after they've had a fling with a foreigner.

Bridget Is it "enlightened"?

Esther Your father is not a racist.

Lol Name me one occasion / where I ——

Bridget Last week. In the *Golden Dragon*.

Lol When?

Bridget When the waiter asked if you wanted wine and you said, "You already took our order, mate. At least I think it was you."

Lol (*holding his arms wide*) Where's the problem?

Daniel returns with a battered old electric fire, complete with a fake log effect on the front, and an extension cable

Esther Here we are!

Lol (*holding his arms out*) Where's the racism / in ——?

Esther (*sotto voce*) Lol.

Daniel unrolls the extension cable during the following. The conversation carries on at whisper-level

Bridget (*smoking*) I cannot describe the colour blue to you if you can't see it.

Lol (*screwing up his face*) What?

Bridget And it's not a "fling". *Is* it?

This comment lands on the carpet and glows

Daniel plugs the log fire in and turns it on. The little whirring convection motor starts and makes the fake logs appear to glow

Esther (*suddenly louder*) I can't tell you the joy, Daniel ... Hasn't it, Lol? Waking up in a morning, hearing your tractors going up and down the Ridgeway.

Daniel smiles politely and hands out wine. Bridget ends up with the Road Runner glass; Adam has the Coke glass; Esther has the Silver Jubilee glass

Smelling that lavender in the air. Now — (*she gestures*) all this with the lambing. I've got this amazing picture now of two young lads suckling lambs in front of a fire.

Daniel Right. Did y' get it from that antiques shop?

There is a pause. Bridget suddenly bursts out laughing

Esther No, I mean — (*tapping her head*) up here. Y'know.

Adam enters with a tiny stool and a tiny bowl of crisps

Adam Oh. Good lad.

Bridget carries on laughing. Esther glares at Bridget. The lads look at her, Adam with a faint smile

Esther (*inspecting her glass*) Oo, now that takes me back. Silver Jubilee. That was a hot summer.

They sit, ending up thus: Daniel on the beanbag, Bridget in the swivel chair, Lol and Esther on the director's chairs, and Adam on the stool. In the centre of them all, as though they've corralled it, is the battered electric fire. The logs flicker. Light plays on their faces

Lol and Esther make eyes at Bridget. Bridget calms to a smile

I was pregnant with you, that summer — (*she taps her nails on the glass and nods*) that's on the glass. (*She nods pointedly at Bridget to admonish her*)
Bridget I've got the Road Runner on my glass.
Esther Oh.
Adam Yeah, sorry about the glasses, it's a bit of / a ——
Lol Hey. Bloody hell. It's a farm.
Bridget (*quietly*) Aye. 'appen it is.

Bridget inspects her glass. Lol looks at her. There is a pause. They all sip wine out of their now-very-noticeably different glasses

Esther (*clapping*) And here we are. The Shellmedines of Sparkbrook meet the Voyseys of Birch Tree Barn. (*She beams*)

Everyone sips again

Is this your first safari party? (*She sips*) We used to have them all the time in Foxhill Grove, didn't we, Lol?

Lol says nothing, woundedly

Adam Is that the bungalow estate?

Esther Development. Lovely bungalows, really.

Lol They are lovely bungalows. / And ——

Esther The *gardens!*

Lol Lovely gardens.

Esther Oh, the gardens are just ——

Lol I mean, nothing like we've got now.

Esther Oh God.

Lol But for a new estate, you know. As it was. And with a little brook running through the back gardens ...

Esther Little stream.

Lol Little bit of a muddy affair. I always said / it ——

Esther *Lol.*

Lol Bit of a shit creek.

Esther *Lol!*

Lol No-o. They're all right! Bloody hell. It was a shit creek, lads. But I fancied a water feature. D'y know what I mean by "water feature"?

Adam W-waterfall?

Lol (*pointing at him*) Perhaps. Perhaps a little waterfall, yes. Or a terrazza, y'know? Widening it out a bit and building / a little (*he gestures*) ——

Esther (*dramatically*) *He never got that far.*

Lol Anyway —— (*He pauses. To Esther*) Wuff.

There is a pause. Adam and Daniel look slightly confused by this noise

(*Dramatically*) I never got that far. Soon as I started working, I'm in bloody casualty.

Esther (*dramatically*) His skin was / completely ——

Lol *Wuff.*

Pause

They did some tests. Turns out the water was contaminated from some farm and that / stream ——

Adam What?

Lol (*dramatically*) That stream, our / little ——

Esther (*even more dramatically*) Our little stream / was ——

Lol *In a minute I'm going to get a spray gun out. I've told y', it's like trying to drive with a dog biting the wheels.*

There is a frosty pause. Bridget looks to her mum. A pause. But Esther surfaces smiling

Esther This is the ideal number for a safari. Three houses. Or four. If it gets up to six, you sort of run out of courses.

Pause

Plus you get: one house ends up doing the main course, and one ends up just doing coffee and mints, and it's not ... (*She gestures*) At least this way it works out even. Inga doing dessert, us doing main course and you doing the hors d'oeuvres.

Adam looks at Daniel

Daniel (*sotto voce*) Fkkknlll.

Daniel hastens out with the tabletop tray

Esther There's just something fabulous about the walking between courses. Isn't there, Lol? And that was round Foxhill Grove, on pavements. Out here is just — organic. It's just "right".

Pause

Adam You say you've got a bigger garden here than before?
Esther Oh yes. We've got a paddock.
Adam A paddock? *Have* you?
Esther I mean nothing compared to here, obviously. You must have ... How much land have you got?
Adam Hundred and sixty acres.
Esther My God.
Adam I mean in me grandad's time it was four hundred odd. Big dairy farm. Big ... (*He waves his hand expansively*) "Sparkbrook herd"——everyone knew Sparkbrook.
Esther Which must be hard to look after, just the two of you? It is ——?
Adam Well, since Dad died.
Esther Neither of you have partners?
Bridget What time are we eating?
Adam Sorry?
Bridget Absolutely famished. All that safari-ing.
Adam Well, it shouldn't be, 1 ... (*Calling*) *Dan?*
Esther I mean to manage that much land must be a nightmare.
Adam Well y'know. Even little bits of land can be trouble. Even little ... Y'know. Paddocks. If they're not regularly maintained. I mean like yours, / say ——

Esther Oh, but ours is a postage stamp compared to this. I mean all the *time* involved, the *hours* ... I don't suppose you get much opportunity to socialize.

Bridget Crisps'd do. Can I see if there's any crisps? (*She rises with the bowl*)

Daniel enters

Daniel Did someone call f ...?

Bridget Coming for some crisps.

Daniel *No!* (*He blocks the door with a movement that is more dramatic than he would have intended*)

Pause

Sorry. I'm at a delicate stage of the er ... The meat is a little bit — (*finding Adam's eyeline; grimly*) *snapping*.

Bridget What?

Esther (*in like a tiger*) Is that a phrase? See, this — I've been talking to Inga about this in the shop. Local phrases. Does "snapping" mean "fresh"?

Daniel (*eyeing to Adam*) Y-yes.

Daniel exits, leaving Bridget unable to go

Esther Well I have to say *we've* found that, haven't we? The freshness? Out here? Of the food? The food's fresher, the air's sweeter but the *people* ...! (*She shakes her head in wonder*) Pardon my language, but I'm going to use the "c" word.

Bridget and Adam look at Esther

People round here are a better (*whispering*) class. (*She does a "high" gesture with her hand*)

Everyone looks at the gesture

Bridget Can I just say here, Adam, they've moved less than a mile.

Esther Bridget, Spain is "less than a mile" from Portugal. I mean Inga's place, "Cornucopia", you wouldn't've got a shop like that selling rural antiques down in Foxhill Grove would you? I mean the thing / is ——

Lol What d'you think of "Zoom-Golf!"?

Pause

Adam Sorry?
Lol "Zoom", then a hyphen, then "golf", then an exclamation mark.

Pause

See Adam, the image of golf in this country ——

Bridget gives a tiny sigh

(*Pouncing on it like a tiger*) Sorry?

There is a slight pause

Esther (*inspecting her glass*) It was such a hot summer. The blackberries.
I remember the blackberries were huge, that year / and ——
Lol I've got two shops, Adam. Male and female. "Lord Of The Links", the
male, and "Ladies On The Links" / which ——
Esther The female.

Lol looks at Esther. She looks away and sips

Lol Which Esther manages. And I'm opening a third for the younger market.
Possibly "Zoom-Golf"! Is it a young word, is it? "Zoom"?
Adam (*after a slight pause*) I — er …
Bridget Do you say "zoom" a lot, Adam? As a young person?

Adam looks at Bridget

You know. D'you get up in the morning and say, "I'm just going to have
a shower. Zoom."

Everyone looks at each other. Pause

Lol Y'see in Portugal it's a younger man's game. Lot of Portuguese lads
play, but they never do much at international level because they're all
twats.
Adam Sorry?
Lol National trait. They're useless. They get attracted to new things, then lose
interest.
Adam Right.
Lol (*waving his arm*) Happens with golf. Y'know? *Women.*
Adam Uh-hu.
Lol I've never been in the national gallery of Portugal but I bet all the
paintings are half-finished.

Adam (*politely*) Ha.
Lol In fact I bet the bloody gallery's still under tarpaulin 'cause halfway
through someone turned up with a case of Stella and a football and that was
it.
Bridget Dad, it's not a young word, OK? That's what his silence is saying.
"Zoom-Golf" on a sign would be phenomenally embarrassing.

A pause. The doorbell goes

Esther (*standing*) Oh that'll be Inga. I'll ... (*She sits*) Oooops.
Adam (*heading for the exit*) What's her name again?
Esther (*bursting to answer the door*) It's Inga. Healey. From the shop. From
"Cornucopia". D'you not know her? I presumed ——

The doorbell goes again

Oh well, shall I? (*She points to the door*) I'll introduce you.

Daniel enters, pinny on

Daniel Is somebody going?
Adam Yes, Esther's — er ——
Esther I'll go!

Esther fair springs off the chair and scuttles out to answer the door

Bridget (*sotto voce*) D'you want a hand?
Daniel Eh?
Bridget I used to work in a kitchen. Obviously it was a Portuguese
kitchen so as Dad'll tell you we never actually finished cooking
anything, / but I ——
Inga (*off*) Mr Voysey?

*Inga enters. She is a well-spoken, well-preserved woman in her early
sixties*

Sorry. Mr Voysey?

Daniel puts his head down and moves behind Adam

Daniel (*sotto voce*) Oh my God.
Inga Your wife has her heel stuck.
Lol (*rising*) Oh for God's sake.

Inga (*going*) In the grating.

Inga exits

Lol follows Inga. Adam frowns at Daniel

Lol (*as he goes*) Can she not step over the bloody thing?

Lol exits

Bridget (*calling after him*) Perhaps that's what it's there for. Keeps out the overdressed. It's the middle class equivalent of a cattle grid.
Adam (*to Daniel*) What?
Daniel (*sotto voce*) Oh shit.
Adam Dan?
Daniel (*sotto voce*) Oh shit. That's her.
Adam Who's her?
Daniel (*crumpling totally*) Oh *shit*.
Adam Whoa boy.
Bridget (*with a half smile*) What's she done?
Daniel Oh, shit, man we are in trouble now. We are in real serious, sorry I'm going to say the word, ff …
Adam *Dan*.
Bridget Christ / almighty.
Daniel (*hitting something*) *Why did we do this meal? Why did we do this stupid sodding / meal?*
Adam What did she do?
Daniel I *knew* it'd be trouble.
Adam *Dan?*
Daniel *I knew it. I bloody / knew* ——
Adam *What did she do?*
Daniel (*pointing towards the front door; dramatically*) She bought our table.

Pause

Bridget I have to say I'm slightly disappointed with that outcome.
Adam I know. That really was building to something bigger, / mate.
Daniel Oh, bigger. You want bigger. OK. OK. I went to that car boot sale, you remember?
Adam I remember / you ——
Daniel I told you a woman had come up, and I had all this stuff laid out on the table / and ——

Adam On the table.

Daniel All Dad's old crap, old saucers and potties and bent spoons, but all Mum's an' all, from way back, all like her wedding rings / an' ——

Adam (*slightly uncomfortable*) Yeah, all right.

Daniel — an' the chain gran left her ——

Adam (*very uncomfortably*) Anyway Dan ——

Daniel — and I was stood there an' this older woman came up and she looked through all Mum's dead precious stuff we didn't want to sell that was out on the table and then said ——

Adam Could she buy the table.

Bridget What table?

Daniel From in here. The kitchen table.

Adam And Dan sold it to her. So hooray.

Daniel No. No, no, no, not "hooray". *Very very not hooray, right?*

Adam Hey, calm down-n.

Daniel (*breathing in, calming himself; a beat*) I did a bad thing.

Bridget Sweetheart. He's really shaking.

Daniel We had no choice, Adam. OK? It was coming into summer, we were forking out hundreds for Warfarin trying to cope with all the rats coming in off the landfill. (*He points*) I'd spent three hours on the phone to bloody Holland trying to find why we hadn't been paid for the spraying, only to find they'd been taken over by some bloody Norwegian company ——

Adam What did you do?

Daniel (*swallowing*) She asked me "How much is the table?" An' suddenly I heard myself saying "Oh, it's more than just a table."

Adam (*after a pause*) What?

Daniel Next thing I know, I'm just flying, man. I'm just making up all kinds of shit about this table.

Adam What?

Daniel All I can remember is this blinding light, this like voice in a light saying "Y' gotta get sixty quid for it, we need the rat poison, y' gotta get sixty quid," and suddenly I'm telling her it's like out of family history this table, like it was made from the boat me grandad used to row across the River Dee to see my gran when they were courting.

Adam *What?*

Daniel *I don't know where it came from.*

Adam (*pointing*) *He lived in Bolton.*

Daniel *I know that.*

Adam *"Rowed across the Dee"?*

Daniel (*wounded*) *Just bastard shut up, Adam.*

Adam (*with slight admiration for this*) That is terrible.

The voices of Inga, Lol and Esther approach

Daniel (*throwing a point at Adam*) You know the story. If they ask. Our grandad — River Dee — courting.

Adam I'm not saying / that.

Daniel *You have to.*

Adam I can't keep that up all night.

Daniel How? Without admitting I'm a liar?

Adam Hey. Who does the cooking round here an' who's got the silver tongue? Just get the hors d'oeuvres.

Daniel *There's no hors d'oeuvres!* I'm trying to make cheesy bacon whirls and the meat is *snapping*, OK? And that's not in the rural Cheshire sense of the word, that's the frozen rigid sense / of ——

Inga (*off*) That's the way.

Bridget (*suddenly*) Come here.

Bridget scoops Daniel off into the kitchen

Inga enters, helping a limping Esther

Inga It is quite narrow. But then they used to be. I bet it's been here as long as the farm, hasn't it, that grid?

Adam By the door? Yes. Well / it ——

Esther Inga, this is Adam. Been here for generations. Ow. I was saying I can't believe you two haven't met.

Inga lowers Esther into her chair

Inga (*looking round and smiling*) Oh, no, well ... No. I'd remember this.

Esther *Isn't* it? Just the most totally, totally organic kind of / farm —— ?

Adam Wine, Inga? (*He pours Inga a glass of wine during the following*)

Inga Eighteenth century?

Adam (*looking at the bottle*) Er ...

Inga The bothy is, certainly.

Esther Sorry?

Inga Where the logs are.

Esther What's that word?

Inga The itinerant labourers, usually Irish navvies, would find summer work on the farms and they'd be accommodated in a "shant" or "bothy". Usually above where the bull was kept.

Esther (*whispering*) "Shant".

Inga And this probably once would've been the kitchen?

Adam It *is* the kitchen.

Inga Oh. Right. But probably there would've been a range in here once?

Esther and Inga share a smile

Esther And a dresser! With a tea service! (*She gestures at the picture she's creating*) Jars of damson gin all lined up!
Adam We ... (*He nods*) Well, there was certainly a cupboard with a large amount of alcohol in it. Ha.
Inga And a big oak table.
Adam (*after a slight pause*) So Inga. Cheers!
Inga Was there? Big oak table?

Bridget enters with crisps

Adam This — is Bridget!
Esther Oh Inga, my daughter. Bridget.
Bridget I've been in / Portugal ——
Esther She's been / in ——
Adam Portugal. (*He nods*) Cheers.

They all sip. Bridget hands the crisps round. Beat

Funny. One of my cousins was saying he'd been to a car boot sale recently and it was amazing. I've never been to one myself. Have you been to one?
Esther I haven't actually. Are they good?
Adam Well he was saying, it's weird, but there's apparently these rules that are generally accepted in er, that, er — (*he takes a slight breath in*) that people talk a load of rubbish and it doesn't matter.
Bridget (*sotto voce, in mock admiration*) Silver ton-ngue!
Esther Sorry?
Adam (*flicking glances at Bridget*) About what they're selling. Part of the fun is that they make things up as part of the fun, and that's all — y'know — part of the fun. D'you find that?
Esther As I say, I haven't been.
Adam No. No. (*Pause*) Do you, Inga?
Inga (*sipping politely*) Wrong person to ask.
Adam Really?
Inga I mean I'm sure, Sunday traders, once in a blue moon ... (*Smiling*) I can't condone that, obviously.
Adam Really?
Inga I deal in antiques, Adam.
Adam Right.
Inga I've a tea service at the moment. Beautiful Victorian tea service with a cake holder. But all that sets that apart from any other Victorian tea

service is the fact that I drove out to Warrington one miserable Thursday afternoon and sat in a dusty terraced room where the clock was ticking louder than the television, and bought that tea service from the family of the last surviving navvy to have worked on the Manchester Ship Canal. (*She smiles*)

There is a pause. No-one speaks

Did there used to be a table in here?

Beat

Adam Yeah. Six foot. Built from a boat my grandad used to row across the River Dee.

Bridget snorts a laugh

Esther Bridget?
Inga Pardon?
Bridget Sorry.
Adam Crisp?
Inga Built from —— ?
Esther *Bridget.*
Bridget Sorry, I'm just … It's such a beautiful story. It's just … (*She has to stop again*) Y'know?
Adam (*covering*) Crisp, Inga?
Esther I mean, I will say you do take things for granted out here, you lads. Growing up out here. A story like that, it's just everyday to you, but people like me, grown up in Runcorn … Isn't it, Inga?

Inga doesn't react; in fact she goes a bit distant, as though she'd just got an earpiece message from the mother ship

Where I grew up, that kind of thing — they'd presume y'd just made it up. But here we are, few miles away, in the country, and it happened. (*She looks to Inga*)
Bridget Absolutely. (*A slight pause*) Was it a big boat, Adam?

Adam's and Bridget's eyes meet. Adam swallows audibly

Adam Quite a big boat, yeah.
Bridget Well, it must've been, to have planks long enough to make a table.
Adam Yeah, well … Yeah.

Bridget (*handing round crisps*) Was he a ferryman by trade?
Adam No.
Bridget But he had access to a boat?

Adam has to restrain a smile during the following

Adam He did.
Bridget Did she live actually on the bank, your gran?
Adam (*after a slight pause*) Her family were shellfish gatherers.
Bridget (*bursting out laughing*) *Were* they? (*She immediately suppresses the laugh*) That's nice. Cockles?
Adam Mussels, cockles. Y'know. Whatever got washed up.
Bridget (*half-laughing now*) Oh, wow. That must've been such a beautiful sight. A lone oarsman sculling across to his love. Guided by little yellow squares of light from the far bank.

Pause. During the following their cheeks ache from resisting smiles

Wasn't there a song they used to sing?
Adam Sorry?
Bridget The River Dee boatmen? Someone told me. I mean obviously you'd know it, obviously, if your *grandad* was one.

Adam has to really bite the laughter back now

(*Clicking her fingers*) There was, wasn't there?
Adam Y-yesss.
Bridget How did it go?

Lol strides in with a golf club

Lol *Who said they don't play golf?*
Esther *Lol! Shush. Adam's going to sing the song of the River Dee Boatmen.*

Adam looks at Bridget, who is looking down, unable to meet his gaze

Adam Erm. I've forgotten it really ...
Esther Oh, no, no, try. Please try. I'd love to hear it. Inga would love to hear it, wouldn't you?

Bridget is sitting with her head down now, suppressing laughter

Adam Well, it was just, er ... Oh God, it just went something like the ... er ... (*He looks up to see if everyone's lost interest, which is his ploy*)

Esther looks at Adam with desperate attention, hanging on his every breath

Er ... (*Growling a "line"*) The R-river Dee ——

Bridget, head down, starts to shake

— is big and wide.

Bridget convulses, but is still silent

The dum dum something ... hrmmm (*pause*) the other side.

Pause

Esther (*shaking her head in wonder*) That is so beautiful.

Bridget stands and exits into the kitchen making a small noise

Lol (*holding up the golf club*) Ta-da! (*He cleans the metal bit of the club with spittle during the following*) Bruchner, would you believe it?
Esther (*referring to Adam's song*) Isn't it, Inga?

Inga has gone oddly quiet

Lol I hate to say this, but the one thing the Germans are good at is steel. (*He holds the club aloft*) Look at that. A nation summed up in a golf club. Efficient, clinical, brutal ...

Daniel enters with some plates on the tabletop

Daniel (*seeing Lol brandishing the club; backing off*) Christ.
Lol Did you know this little gem was in your shed? (*He spit-cleans the club again*)
Daniel Yeah, it's er ... Dad found it up in some phone wires. The vet sometimes uses it.
Lol (*re-licking his fingers*) Does he play?
Daniel If the umbilical gets wrapped round the lamb's neck in the womb.

Lol's attitude to the club suddenly changes

Adam Daniel. This is Inga. Inga, this is my brother, Daniel.
Inga (*nodding, grimly*) Oh yes. Yes, *I* see.
Daniel Pardon?

Inga (*nodding; quieter*) I see now.
Adam We were just saying how the old kitchen table was a piece of Cheshire history.

Bridget swoops in behind Daniel, carrying a plate of bacon and cheese

Bridget And here we are with another. Genuine Cheshire Tollycurney.

They all look at her, totally lost, Daniel in particular

The traditional dish of North Cheshire. (*She hands a piece to Lol*)

Lol sits

Strips of bacon and very cold cheese. And this dates back to days of the cheese barges coming up from the south swapping pigmeat with the Irish barges, and like the wrapping of the cold cheese in the warm bacon symbolized the warming of a friendship.

Pause

Esther (*swallowing; breathlessly*) God, I love this county.
Adam (*nodding, smiling*) Yes. That's right. That's right. In fact there was a song, wasn't / there?
Bridget No.
Esther (*clapping*) Oh, well, Mrs Cheshire History will know! No-one better to ask! (*She turns, at the top of her social game, beaming, to Inga*) She's right here sitting with us. Do you know the Tollycurney song, Inga?

Pause. Unexpectedly, Inga stands

Inga Well. (*Grabbing her coat*) I hope you've had your fun, you vindictive little snake-pit of bastards.

Inga turns and exits into the front door corridor

Pause. Everyone looks off into the corridor

Esther (*turning back, beaming*) Yes-s. And it's just — "the rowing across the Dee". You see, people don't know about that. That's what ... I mean didn't I always / say ——
Lol (*sotto voce*) What was that?

All the others look where Inga went

Esther Nothing you pick up is just a thing, is it? Everything's a story. Everything's a story.

Pause

Don't you think? Everything? (*She peters out*)

Silence. Deadly, horrible silence

Adam does a "bloody hell" face to Bridget and goes after Inga

Lol (*to Esther*) Well, go on, then.

Esther looks at him

You too. This was your bloody idea, this safari.

Esther looks at Bridget

Go on, Daktari. See what's happened.

Esther follows Adam off

Everyone looks at everyone else

Bridget Are you going?
Esther (*off*) Ow. Ohh-h (*Calling*) Lol.
Lol (*rising*) Oh, for Christ's *sake*.

Lol exits

This leaves Daniel and Bridget round the Tollycurney

Daniel Shouldn't've done that.
Bridget What?
Daniel (*quietly*) Looked like we were laughing at her.
Bridget Why does it bother you?
Daniel Not surprised she walked out. (*Looking at Bridget; more heatedly*) It doesn't bother you? She's gone away 'cause she thinks I'm a vindictive bastard? 'Cause I made up a story about my kitchen table and she fell for it an' spent sixty quid falling for it and we were all —

"Ha ha, stupid Inga, believing old crap like River Dee boat songs and
bloody — Tollycurney" ...
Bridget (*after a slight pause*) It wasn't just you. I think it was bastards plural.

Daniel tidies up the glasses during the following

I spend my life lying. (*She lights another cigarette*) I'm lying now. (*She
blows out smoke, coolly*)

Daniel tidies

A real big one. A real whopper.
Daniel It can't be that serious if y'r prepared to tell someone y've only just
met. 'Cause that's what y' want. Y'r wanting me to ask now, aren't y'? (*He
faffs with the bacon*)
Bridget Top Tollycurney. (*She eats some*) That's what they say, isn't it? Big
lies want to come out. They want fame.

Daniel continues to faff with the bacon

I've told my parents / that ——
Daniel *Don't tell me.* If you wanna lie, don't make me have to carry it round
as well 'cause I can't do it. I will let you down. (*He is suddenly fired*) I will
let you down.

Bridget smiles at this guy

Adam comes in with a wry smile

Adam (*sotto voce, gesturing "gone"*) Vam-oosh. (*He pulls an "oo-er" face
in the silence*)

Esther enters, pale, followed by Lol

*Everyone stands round limply as people must stand after witnessing an
assassination*

Pause

Lol Well. I think it's safe to say you won't be getting a discount on that tea
service.
Esther *That's not why I did it.*
Daniel (*embarrassed*) Anyway-y ...

Esther I go there, Lol, sometimes I don't even buy things. I just talk.
Daniel (*sotto voce*) Can we stop —— ?
Adam Yeah, come on. Tollycurney's supposed to be a symbol of peace.
Daniel (*to Adam, in a vicious whisper*) *Will you shut up about sodding Tollycurney?*

Pause. Cheese melts on the plate

Lol (*nodding at the food*) Well, let's have some, anyway, lad. We can't afford to miss out on starters if the pudding's just done a runner.
Bridget (*in a heavy Yorkshire accent*) Aye, lad. Gerrit out on us plates.
Lol Sorry, d'you have a problem with me saying the word "lad"?
Bridget You don't say it. You roll in it to acquire the scent.
Adam (*offering Tollycurney to Lol*) Lol?

Lol takes some Tollycurney and eats it. There is a pause

Lol Anyway. Great idea for a dinner party, love. Next time perhaps we could have some vegetarians round for a cockfight.
Bridget *Dad?*
Lol Eh, this isn't my fault. I didn't make Helga go off in a huff.
Adam Helga?
Bridget He knows it's Inga.
Lol Look ——
Bridget I have to warn you before the evening's over he'll go through Helga, Lottie, Gretchen / Grunhilda ——
Lol Can I just say here, lads, Bridget has recently had a holiday romance with a foreigner.
Bridget Sod off.
Lol You know? And in the same way that if she'd gone to Cornwall she'd've come back a massive fan of pasties —— ?
Bridget Don't try to get them on your side.
Lol Well they're not on yours, sugar plum. They're farmers. You're not gonna get them wearing "I heart Europe" T-shirts, not when ... (*He suddenly turns to Daniel for back-up*) What's your income?
Adam What?
Lol This month. What are y' doing this month?
Adam Spraying.
Lol Yeah, but which crop?
Adam The tip.
Lol What?
Adam We've got a contract to maintain the landfill site. The council tip. Where they've made it into a hill. We look after that. (*He pauses*)

Lol is aghast

Used to be wheat and barley. Called the "Fifty Acre".

There is a pause while Lol takes in the full horror of this

Lol *Y' see?* Our British Cheshire farmers are mowing a *tip*, while (*gesturing*)
Costas, right — (*pointing*) Enrico bloody "three goats" Gonzales gets a
subsidy to sit on his arse outside a café playing draughts with his group of
one-toothed mates.
Esther (*pointing suddenly*) *That's why she went.*
Lol What?
Esther *That's why she went off. Her parents were German.*
Lol Eh?
Esther "A nation summed up in a golf club. Efficient, clinical, brutal."
Daniel Her parents / were —— ?
Esther Were German, Lol. Which is what she told me once when I was
talking to her once in her shop. When we were becoming friends.

Esther exits down the corridor to the front door

There is the sound of a door slamming. Lol looks at Adam and Daniel

Lol Tell y' what. There's gradually getting more and more Tollycurney for
us, in't there, lads?

Pause. Bridget stares at him

(*Responding to the stare*) What?
Bridget Your wife is walking down a dark road.
Lol It's the countryside.

Bridget rises

Oh all right, all right. Jesus. I'll go and stop her being — maliciously
nuzzled by a cow. (*To Adam*) Is there a toilet before / I ——?
Bridget (*moving off after her mum*) Oh for ff-ff ...

Bridget exits

Lol (*calling after Bridget*) *You want me to do it in a hedge? I'm not bloody
French.*
Adam It's down on the left.

Lol heads for the indoor corridor

Lol (*as he passes, nodding at the Tollycurney*) Put that in a bag. We'll re-heat it at our place.

Lol exits down the indoor corridor

Daniel and Adam are alone

Daniel (*sotto voce*) No way ——
Adam I know.
Daniel (*pointing*) — am I going ——
Adam OK, / OK.
Daniel — anywhere near ——
Adam Dan.
Daniel You know who he is. You know who he bloody is?
Adam (*after a pause*) Yeah.
Daniel It's like the spirit's come out of the grave.
Adam Don't start talking / like ——
Daniel No, but this is what happens. That's what worries me. This can happen.
Adam What?
Daniel Y'can get these spiritual-like — echoes.
Adam No you can't.
Daniel In the psych-y ... Spiritual — *y'can*. Where an unhappy spirit / just ——
Adam There is no such thing as an "unhappy spirit".
Daniel Oh, I think there is. I think Dad died unhappy.
Adam How d'you know?
Daniel Because you *told me*.

There is a slight pause

Adam Yeah. Well ——
Daniel He apologized for what he did to me, then shot himself. Now even if, on his way to the ground, he started to sing something from *Showboat*, that's still not gonna count as a "happy" death.
Adam (*grabbing him*) A happy death is where you get peace and show remorse, OK, Dan, and he did that.

There is a slight pause

I was there. You weren't.

There's the sound of a toilet flushing, off

Daniel What are y' gonna say?
Adam I just ... Let me ... (*He thinks for a few beats, then gestures*) Silver tongue, remember?

Lol emerges from the indoor corridor

Lol Right. Come on, lads. Bring some of that Tollycurney.
Adam Lol?
Lol (*grandly*) Main course awaits at Birch Tree Barn.
Adam Listen, / Lol ——
Lol Esther's Hawaiian Chicken.
Adam *Lol, I'm not sure / that we ——*
Lol Also when we get there I want a word about this paddock.

Lol exits

Adam turns to Daniel

Music: "Swingin' Safari" by The Bert Kaempfert Orchestra

Daniel looks at the Tollycurney. He sighs. He picks some up. He heads towards the front door

Adam stops Daniel and hugs him like a soldier resigned to going over the top

Then they both walk out of the door towards the main course

Black-out

ACT II
The Entrées

The new conservatory of the Voysey's barn conversion

There are two exits, one to the yard and garden via french windows and the other into the kitchen and the rest of the house. The room is dominated by a six-by-three foot table covered with a red gingham cloth on which are set places for six people

When the Act begins, the room is bathed in moonlight. Music plays: the insistent strains of "Swingin' Safari"

Esther hobbles in, one leg higher than the other due to her shoe's missing heel

"Swingin' Safari" stops

Esther breathes in, heavily. There is a silent pool of pause in the moonlight of the conservatory as she takes a moment to compose herself

Suddenly a floodlight comes on outside, of similar ferocity to a Stalag 7 searchlight

Esther winces slightly. She turns on the overhead lights and exits into the kitchen, removing her coat. The kitchen light comes on

Lol enters from the garden

Lol Bloody ridiculous. What's the point of having a security light that only comes on if you jump up and down waving your arms in the air?

No response from the kitchen

You know?

No response

It rather leaves us having to hope we only get burgled by someone who, in the process of burgling us, sees someone that he knows.

No response

(*Sighing*) We're only one down.

Esther enters carrying a salt miners' lantern with a lighted candle in it

Esther We shouldn't have that on. Can you take that tablecloth off?
Lol We're only one down.
Esther *They* didn't bother with tablecloths. We shouldn't.
Lol We're only / one ——
Esther It's obviously not a true country thing. Lol, America was "only one down" when Kennedy was assassinated.

Esther removes one place setting and heads into the kitchen

Lol I hope you're not putting Inga in the same bracket as John F. Kennedy.

No response

The searchlight goes off. Light spills in from the kitchen. The salt lantern flickers

During the following Lol moves the place settings on to chairs to facilitate removal of the tablecloth

D'you think they get on? Bridget and whatsit? Them lads? D'you think there's any ... Y'know? Animal whatsit?

Pause

Look, will you stop acting like you've been dumped by some bloody childhood pal. "Inga's a friend. I like her." She's — bollocks. She's a bloody shopkeeper, that's what she is.

Esther returns with two more flickering salt miners' lanterns

Esther Not everyone is like you, Lol. Can you move that cloth?
Lol (*pointing*) Ten per cent.
Esther The cloth?
Lol You were not inviting a person to this dinner party. You were inviting a potential ten per cent discount.
Esther Lol ——
Lol That was not a person that disappeared down that lane. That was ten per

cent of a tea service belonging to the last surviving navvy on the Manchester Ship Canal.

Esther carries on, ignoring him

That is a couple of sideplates in a huff.
Esther (*gently*) D'you want to make friends out here?
Lol She was a shopkeeper, my darling.
Esther And do they not bleed, shopkeepers?
Lol They ... No. Not as much.
Esther (*sotto voce*) Oh, for ——
Lol Because ...

Esther removes a chair and exits into the kitchen with it

Because, if y'd like to listen — (*calling*) and it's not their fault, but as soon as you elect to be a shopkeeper, everyone else in your life becomes a potential customer. End of story.

Esther emerges with another salt miners' lamp

Friendship gets mixed up with the notion of prey, OK? I know. I am one. She was becoming your friend in the same way a clever fox gets pally with an old bantam.

Pause

Esther Thank you.

Bridget appears at the french windows. She has some Tollycurney with her

Bridget She's not here, then?

Esther heads for the kitchen. Bridget comes into the room, taking off her jacket. She eats some Tollycurney

Lol Did them security lights come on?

Lol exits past Bridget into the darkened yard again

Bridget She wasn't just leaving to get a head start?
Esther (*looking at Bridget's hands*) Is that grease? You've been eating —— ?

Bridget (*waving her fingers, her mouth full*) Mm-mg.

Adam appears at the french windows, also eating Tolleycurney

Esther (*seeing Adam*) Adam-m!

Adam comes into the room

(*Heading for the kitchen, smiling*) Oh, I'll just get you some kitchen roll.

Esther exits

Adam (*his mouth full*) That is damn fine Tollycurney.
Bridget (*licking her fingers*) I upset your brother, y' know.
Adam Mg?
Bridget Apparently.
Adam Dan?
Bridget With the Tollycurney. He was a bit narked. I'm surprised you both came on.
Adam (*after a slight pause*) Yeah. Well.
Bridget Glad you did, though.
Adam (*with a wry smile*) Good.
Bridget (*with a wry smile*) Wouldn't've got introduced to that nice bloke otherwise. What was his name? In the lane?
Adam Y'r only impressed 'cause he had two shotguns.
Bridget He's a farmer as well, I take it?
Adam (*with a slight sneer*) Big Dave is indeed a farmer, yes. Except unlike us, Big Dave is rolling in it.
Bridget (*wryly*) He's a very good farmer?
Adam He's a farmer who sold four of his barns to be a candle workshop and consequently now owns a satellite-guided combine harvester.
Bridget Get off.
Adam Straight up. That thing was being guided round fifty acres of Cheshire by something out beyond Saturn. All Dave does is follow it round shooting rats that get freaked by the gangster rap playin' on the stereo.
Esther (*off*) Bridget, the lager's in the bothy.
Adam (*sotto voce*) Anyway. What would Victor say if he know you were eyeing up farmers?
Bridget *Vitor.*
Esther (*off*) Bridget?
Adam (*smiling, wagging a finger, doing a voice*) There'll be ter-wubble.

Bridget smiles. A beat

Bridget What did she …?
Adam "The lager's in the bothy".
Bridget What's that, a Cheshire folk song?
Adam I think she means the shed.
Esther Bridg / et?
Bridget (*louder, heading for the french windows*) Yeah, yeah.

Daniel enters through the french windows

Daniel (*sotto voce, with a weak smile*) Hi.

Bridget passes Daniel and exits through the french windows

(*Turning on Adam*) I want to go home.
Adam D'you want a beer?
Daniel I want to go home is what I want.
Adam (*calling*) *Beer for Dan as well, please.*
Daniel I've just carried him, Adam. I've just … (*He points*) Did you enjoy talking to the young girl? I've just been carrying her father on my shoulders round the farmyard. Is that OK?
Adam Why?
Daniel Because the whole family are round the effing twist.
Adam Dan. *Dan.* (*He takes Daniel's face in hands*) Get through this one night, eighty quid a month for life.
Daniel *How* much?
Adam I'm gonna start at a hundred, mate.
Daniel *For mowing a paddock?*
Adam Silver tongue. Makes eighty seem a climb-down. Ha hargh. (*He taps his nose*) Oh yes. I've seen *Wall Street.*
Daniel Adam, we only get sixty quid for spraying a bloody forty acre landfill.
Adam Does he know that?
Daniel That's not the ——
Adam Does (*he points in the absent Lol's direction*) Jack Nicklaus know that?
Daniel It's far too much / money ——
Adam Eighty quid. Just think, eighty quid a month. That paddock … (*He chucks Daniel's cheek*) Oh g … mmm … get through this evening, that paddock is cinema, Dan. It's satellite television. It's satellite television.
Daniel It's food.
Adam Food.
Daniel Survival.
Adam Food, survival, satellite television … That paddock is our field of dreams. (*He clasps Daniel's face in his hands*)

Lol enters

Lol Bastard security light, y' can't see a bloody thing. (*He points towards the yard*) Anyway, that's the paddock. (*Proudly*) That's where I'm building the swimming pool.
Esther (*off*) *Lol?*
Lol (*heading for the kitchen*) Coming. (*To Daniel and Adam*) Have a beer.

Lol exits

Daniel and Adam stare after Lol. Pause

Daniel (*turning to the french windows*) Good-night. (*He moves to exit*)

Bridget enters with two bottles of beer, blocking Daniel's way

Bridget Two beers. I'll get an opener.

Bridget whips off the gingham tablecloth in one move and exits to the kitchen

Daniel (*calling after Bridget and quietly putting his beer down*) It's all right, I think actually we're going to make — argh! (*He jerks his hand away from the table as though electrocuted*)

Daniel and Adam stare at the table as if at a recently-revealed corpse. Pause. Adam leans in towards the table. Pause

There's a God.
Adam (*sotto voce*) Don't.
Daniel I don't mind dying if it all goes black. I don't want there to be a God. You didn't kill him, did you?
Adam What?
Daniel Dad. You didn't shoot him. You would've told me if you'd shot him?
Adam Just calm down.
Daniel No. You *wouldn't* tell me. You *did* shoot him and we're being punished an' it's like that film where they kill that sea-lion thing and it doesn't die. It keeps turning up outside their tent.
Adam Dan ——
Daniel (*slightly zombified*) What's it called?
Adam Sit down.
Daniel That Australian film where you laughed all the way through and I couldn't sleep for a bastard fortnight.

Adam It just looks like / it ——

Daniel *It is it. It's it.* It's ... It's ... (*He points*) There's the obscenity I carved with my sweetcorn holder during Easter dinner in 1992.

Daniel Look, lots of tables have things carved in / them.

Daniel Not the holes! Not ... *Don't treat me like a kid.* That's the holes! There! (*He slams his way round the table*) There! There! How many oak tables do you know that have those sodding holes in them?

Adam So *what?*

Daniel So why has she bought it, Adam? You don't buy a table full of holes.

Adam Well / she ——

Daniel Normally. No-one does. This is meant. This is arranged. We're going to eat off a crime scene.

Adam Don't start.

Daniel We're being punished. Well *I* am.

Adam For what?

Daniel 'Cause I felt pleased. When you told me he was dead ... In fact, no, I actually thought, what I actually thought was "*Yesss.*"

Adam You had every right.

Daniel That's not what you're supposed to say when your father dies, is it? "*Yesss*".

Adam Yeah, well, as a father you're not supposed to set about your son with a golf club / when ——

Daniel He'd apologized.

Adam —— when you're pissed which, can I remind you, he'd done that morning.

Daniel He'd repented. He'd bloody shot himself in remorse and I said "Yesss". And now I'm going to have to eat off the table that he shot himself on and I ca ...

Esther walks in with kitchen roll

Daniel stops dead

Esther Sorry?

Adam Just saying how lovely the table is.

Esther (*as if the sun has come out*) Oh my table! My table, my table, my table! I just ... Oh. (*She strokes the table, almost putting her head down on it*) It was the first thing we bought. We thought we'd wait a couple of months before choosing a table for the conservatory, but then we saw this and that was it, you know? (*She beams*) Well, I mean it had to be, really, didn't it? Good Lord. You don't turn down a genuine Cheshire Buttyball table when you find one. (*She arranges the table. Under her breath*) Nowww, if this goes he-re ...

Adam and Daniel look at each other for a good five seconds. Esther lays out the plates and the rest of the place settings during the following

Adam A what table, sorry?
Esther You know. The parlour game.

Adam and Daniel look at Esther

The old Cheshire parlour game. Buttyball. You must have heard of it?

Adam and Daniel slowly shake their heads

You've not—? Oh that's ... (Calling) Lol? You've really not ...? Oh well that's ... It's rare. In a shop like (*she points*) "Cornucopia", that's what separates your run-of-the-mill two hundred quid kitchen table from one like this which is worth two and a half thousand.

Esther exits

(*Calling, off*) Lol, have you got those Buttyball balls?

Adam and Daniel do not move. At all. They stare at the two and a half thousand pound table

Bridget enters from the kitchen, with her own beer

Bridget OK with bottles? D'you want a glass? (*She opens Adam's and Daniel's bottles*)

Adam and Daniel don't seem to notice what Bridget is doing

(*Moving to the french windows*) God, you do get the smell of the country up here, I have to say. (*She breathes in*) Fantastic, that lavender. Is that lavender?

Adam and Daniel still do not move. At all. They still stare at the two thousand pound table

(*Turning*) That smell? (*She looks at Adam and Daniel*) What's happened?
Adam (*quietly*) How much did they pay for this table?
Bridget (*shrugging*) I was abroad. I dunno. Quite a lot, I think. But it's ... There's something special about it. It's got a special name. (*She clicks her fingers*) It's / a ——

Daniel ⎱ (*together; dully soporific*) Buttyball.
Adam ⎰
Bridget Buttyball table, that's it. *You* probably had one, didn't you?
Daniel ⎱ (*together; nodding slowly*) Mmm.
Adam ⎰
Bridget What happened to yours?
Adam It's here.

Pause

Bridget You're kidding? (*She pauses*) They bought it?
Daniel For two and a half thousand pounds.

There is a slight pause as Bridget cottons on

Bridget And-d you sold it to Inga for ... ?
Daniel Sixty.
Bridget Uh-huh.

Pause

Adam (*calm, calm*) Which, y'know ... Hey. It's not all profit. The petrol getting it from the car boot sale to her place ...
Bridget Ten pounds.
Adam And the beeswax. 'Cause she'll've re-waxed / it ——
Daniel Two-ninety a tin.
Adam And all the heating in the shop, you know. Her net profit's coming down to about — (*he slams his hand on the table*) *two thousand four hundred.*
Esther (*off*) Everything OK?

Pause

Adam (*turning*) Did you not know it was a Buttyball table?
Daniel (*turning to Adam*) What the hell d'y—? "Did I not—?" I don't know what bloody Buttyball is. Do you know?
Adam I wasn't selling the bloody table.
Daniel *I* wasn't till she offered to buy it.
Adam Well ——
Daniel I can't help if Mrs Sodding Bygone Cheshire Expert turns up.

Pause

Adam My God. He even managed to screw this up for us, didn't he?
Bridget Who?
Adam We might've thought about taking it to an antiques shop if it hadn't got bullet holes in it. Y'd never think y'd get anything for a table with bullet holes in it.
Bridget Bullet holes?
Adam An' if it *hadn't* got bullet holes in it, and if we'd taken it to a shop ——
Daniel Don't.
Adam — can you imagine what a Buttyball table would be worth ——
Daniel Don't.
Adam — *without* bullet holes?

There is a slight pause

Bridget (*as if on glass*) What happened here to be making bullet holes?
Daniel Dad shot himself.
Bridget (*jerking her hand away*) Oh my God.

Pause. The lads stare into the middle distance

(*Sotto voce, her hand over her mouth*) Oh my God, oh my God. That's terrible.
Adam I know. I could've gone to Ibiza.
Bridget No I mean / your ——
Adam (*dropping his head to the table*) I could've gone to Ibiza-a.
Bridget I mean your dad. That he shot — ? Oh God, I'm so sorry ... I mean what happens? With something like that? How d'you cope with something like that?
Daniel I wasn't there.
Adam (*not looking at Bridget*) You put a jug down. You put a jug down so the blood coming down through the holes doesn't mark the lino. (*A slight pause*) If it's me dad, you bother about the lino.

Pause. Daniel his has head in his hands. Adam stares at the evening sky through the conservatory roof. Bridget stares wide-eyed at both of them. Tick. Tock

Lol bursts in. He is carrying a white ball the size of a large marble and what look like four small putters that dwarves might play golf with

Lol Right! Buttyball! (*He holds up the ball*) This — I mean — (*he chops one hand into the other*) amazing. We wanted a farmhouse table. (*He hands out*

the little putters) You know. "Barn". All that. Y've gotta have one of these
tables. I mean, we could've had a repro but then suddenly, *suddenly* to find
a Buttyball table — for someone involved in golf, it's just like — ha!

*Lol sets up the game during the following. Daniel and Adam have little
putters thrust into their hands*

See what it is, historically not everyone had access to a golf course.
'Specially not rural Cheshire. So what developed was like a "home-golf"
you could play *in your kitchen!* Y'know? On your table. (*He waves his little
club*) Little club, made from wood carried in the butties pulled by barges,
OK? "Butties"? "Buttyball"? And then look! This is brilliant.

Lol gathers the others round the table

Holes! See? Here — and here — two more there andd-d there. Now they'd
make these we think with sheep-shearing implements — them big long
bloody things — and you'd sheep-shear your holes, an' they'd all be worth
a different number of points. The nearer the edge, the higher, 'cause if y'go
off the edge y've lost your entire score. OK? (*He looks at the others and
beams*) Can't you just imagine? Nineteenth century. Winter's night.
Ruddy faces from turning God's earth. Crimson jars of damson gin on the
dresser. Fire in the hearth. The farmer and his sons, the beating heart of rural
Cheshire, playing Buttyball. (*He starts to tee up, but then turns to point with
the club for emphasis*) An' what chance, eh? She only started telling us
about Buttyball after I mentioned me line of business. If I hadn't mentioned
golf to Inga, I'd never've known this game existed! (*He tees off and misses*)
Ooo! Close!

Esther comes in bearing a dish of Hawaiian chicken

Esther Clear the green! Clear the fairway!

*Esther puts the dish down and dims the overhead lights so the room is lit just
by the sultry glow from the salt-miners' lamps. There is a little moment at
which one could say "Ahh" at the scene. Then the blindingly bright security
light comes on outside*

(*Wincing*) Oh. Lol. The light, the / light.
Lol How's that come on? (*He heads into the yard*) Why the hell's that come
on now?

Lol exits

Esther (*wincing*) Main course! About time, everybody says.

Bridget, Adam and Daniel put down their buttybats and sit at the table. Esther doles out the chicken during the following, oblivious to the fact that everyone is stupefied by the airport-runway-scale light

You've had a quick game? It's a beautiful thing, isn't it? To think? (*She passes a plate to Adam*) Adam? The Buttyball? Isn't it? All those years. You can just imagine. (*She passes a plate to Daniel*) Daniel? Farmers. Coming in from the fields. Faces all ruddy. Gathering round this table. Crimson jugs of damson gin on the mantelpiece. Playing Buttyball.

The light suddenly goes off. There's a clang outside

Lol (*off*) *Shit.*
Esther The beating heart of rural Cheshire.

Lol enters and stands in the doorway

Lol God. *God. Bollocks.* If I didn't know better, I'd think whoever wired that up was taking the piss.
Esther *Lol.*
Lol (*pointing back into the yard*) You know it goes off as soon as anyone walks in front of it?
Esther (*holding out a plate to Lol*) Lol?

Lol exits

Lol (*off*) If I've dented that bloody milk churn …
Esther *Lol, I'm serving the chick …* (*She winces at Adam for approval*) It's chicken. I thought that'd probably be — (*nodding*) not too spicy.

Adam and Daniel can't quite make their responses form into words

Daniel Hrmmgrrrm.

Lol clanks in with a large green milk churn. The churn has the words "Birch Tree Barn" enamelled on to it but as yet we cannot see them

Lol I have y'know. I've bloody dented that.
Esther *Don't bring it in.*
Lol See?
Esther *Lol.*

Lol You don't seem very concerned, sweetheart. These are supposed to be
the bloody main feature of the drive, these. (*To Adam*) We're having a row
of 'em up the drive with ivy growing out. Thirty of 'em. Just got 'em back
from the enamellers. Look. (*He turns the churn to show the lettering to the
others*) "Birch Tree Barn".
Esther That's what we've decided to call it.
Lol (*running his finger over the name*) In enamel.
Esther It's never had a name, obviously, just being a barn, so we thought
we'd name it after the tree in the paddock.
Lol (*running his finger over the name again*) Not painted, that. Enamelled.
Nine hundred quid, but it's worth it.
Esther Organic name.
Lol Y'didn't see, probably, 'cause of the bloody Portuguese security light,
but thirty of 'em — (*gesturing*) up the drive. In gold. "Birch Tree Barn".
Daniel (*sotto voce*) It's an ash.

Everyone looks at Daniel.He takes a sparrowy bite of chicken

In the paddock. Not a birch.

There is a pause. Everyone eats a few mouthfuls in silence. Chew. Chew

Lol Probably have to come down for the swimming-pool anyway. (*Pause.
Chew chew*) It's an ash?
Esther (*smiling*) We could change it.

Pause

We could change the name.
Lol (*sotto voce*) Never mind.
Esther Couldn't we? It's only money.
Lol Never mind.
Esther (*after a pause*) We could change the name / to ——
Lol *To what.*

Daniel jumps and drops his fork

Esther Well ——
Lol Tell me to what, so it'd be called what? To what / would you —— ?
Esther Well / I don't know ——
Lol Tell me. Go on.
Esther "Ash Tree / Barn".
Lol "Ash Tree". Good. That's nice. We live in "Ash Tree". That's nice.

Esther Oh, I see.

Lol We live in an ash tray.

Esther OK, Lol.

Lol We live actually in an ash tray.

Esther Potatoes?

Lol That's "Ash Tree Barn" next to "Fag End Cottage" up past "Urinal Mews".

Esther *Lol, I get the p* ... (*She checks her volume and smiles*) He's always like this when he hurts himself. Isn't he, Bridget? Hit his leg on a railing at EuroDisney and / oh my God.

Lol (*quietly*) He was in a fibreglass head.

Esther The mouthful he gave that character.

Lol He was in a fibreglass head. He couldn't hear a bloody thing. (*A slight pause*) And he was French. (*Pause*) Is it an ash? Is it really ash?

Everyone carries on eating in silence a few mouthfuls

Ffffuck.

Esther *Lol.*

Bridget puts her cutlery down

(*To Bridget*) What's the matter?

Bridget (*arranging her cutlery*) I'm not actually that hungry.

Lol *What?*

Bridget (*sotto voce*) Sorry.

Esther Are you / feeling —— ?

Lol 'Cause it's English?

Esther What's the matter?

Bridget Nothing.

Lol She doesn't eat English food any more, lads. She won't eat chicken, but she'd eat bloody chipboard if it had an olive on it.

Bridget (*gesturing to her wine glass*) Is there / any —— ?

Esther *The damson gin!*

Bridget (*heading out*) I'll get it.

Bridget exits

Esther Nearly forgot the damson gin!

Lol (*calling after Bridget*) Listen it was English, this chicken, but politically it was very pro-Europe. The bloke at the abattoir said when he opened it up it had "Calais" written on its ... Eh, that'll be the next thing ——

Esther (*snapping; sotto voce*) Will you not talk about abattoirs?

Lol Why? Crying out loud … (*Pointing with his fork*) They're farmers, love!
   They're not like you. They deal in blood. This is the countryside. The
   countryside is blood.
Daniel (*sotto voce*) I don't like blood.

*Esther does a "told you" roll of the eyes at Lol. They carry on eating a few
mouthfuls in silence*

Lol How d'you get on at the abattoir then?
Esther (*a low grunt: "Shut up"*) Hrrmm.
Lol Must be like the bloody Somme in them places.
Esther (*a higher grunt: "bloody shut up"*) Mneek.
Adam We don't go. We just send 'em off. They go off in a truck and come
   back in bags. For us it's more like Vietnam.

   Bridget enters with an earthenware jug. She puts it down on the table

Bridget Damson gin.
Daniel *Aaargh.*

Daniel recoils from the table as though a ghost has just appeared

Esther *What's the matter? What's the matter?* He's stopped talking about
   blood.
Daniel (*taking deep breaths*) D'y have a toilet?
Bridget (*pointing*) On the right.

   Daniel goes

Pause

Esther (*turning to Lol*) *Are you doing it deliberately?*
Lol Eh?
Bridget (*to Adam*) What's the matter with him?
Esther It's your bloody *father.*

   Esther drops her cutlery pointedly and stomps out

Adam Where did you get that jug?
Lol Sorry?
Adam The jug.
Lol That jug?
Adam The jug.

Lol Same place as the table. Inga "You vindictive bastards" Healey.
Bridget Why?
Adam What have you put in it?
Lol Well, it's y'r damson gin, isn't it? Your proper rural damson gin.
Bridget Why?
Adam That's fine. No, that's OK. OK. (*Pause*) You've cleaned it well,
    haven't you?
Bridget (*recoiling, scraping his chair back, and standing*) *Oh my God.*

Lol recoils, scraping his chair back, and stands too

Lol *What*?

Adam stares at the jug

    What?
Bridget It's not *the* jug?
Lol Eh?
Adam Probably not.
Lol What jug?
Adam Has it got a stamp on the bottom saying "Reject"?

*Bridget lifts the jug like a severed head and looks at the bottom. She breathes
out in relief*

Bridget No.
Adam That's it, then.
Bridget Aargh. (*She drops the jug as a reflex*)

*Deep red damson gin gushes over the table. It drops through the Buttyball
holes*

    Esther races in

    What on earth … ? *Oh* ——
Adam It's practically the only thing that wasn't. It was a wedding present.

*Esther pushes up her sleeves and throws her arms on to the table to stop the
red liquid spilling off the sides*

Esther *Kitchen roll?* Don't just stand there, Lol, put something underneath.
    For God's sake. I don't believe ——

Daniel enters, pale

Daniel Sorry about that. I'm fine now.

Esther rears up and opens her arms, now stained elbow-deep with red liquid

Esther Oh, Daniel, I'm sorry.

Daniel faints to the ground

Bridget Daniel! (*She flies to him*)
Lol (*to Esther*) *What are you trying to do, love?*
Esther *Oh, says he.*
Bridget Water!
Esther He's suddenly concerned about our guests.

Bridget rests Daniel's head in her lap during the following

Bridget For God's / *sake* ...
Lol What's with this bloody jug?
Adam You don't need to know. / It's ——
Lol Was it stolen?
Esther (*theatrically*) He is suddenly concerned / about our guests.
Lol I paid a hundred and fifty quid for that.
Esther (*snatching up the lamps*) The man / who ——
Bridget Look, for Christ's sake, it's the jug Adam used to collect the blood
from his father's head after he shot himself on this table.

*There is a pause. Adam, Lol and Esther look at the table. Esther stands, inert,
with a lamp in either hand. During the following, Lol finishes his meal*

Daniel blinks and comes round, head resting on Bridget's thigh

Esther (*dully, on autopilot*) These lamps were used down the salt mines.

No-one reacts. The security light comes on. No-one moves. It goes off again

Everybody just tell me. Is this dinner party recoverable?

*They all slowly look at Esther. The gravity of the situation suddenly
galvanizes her into a spasm of sweet efficiency*

Of course it is. Daniel's come round so that's fine and Lol sit and so Adam,
that's fascinating, that really is ... This actually ... By a charming
coincidence, we've bought the very table where your father shot hims ...

Oh my —— (*She drops her head on to the table*) —*God-d.*

Lol, who has finished his meal, puts the plate to the middle of the table

Lol (*after a pause*) Do you think it would be fair to conclude there's no such thing as Buttyball? (*He picks up one of the tiny golf clubs and looks at it*) I asked her did she have any original Buttyball clubs? (*He turns the club in his hands*) She said she'd use her "network of dealers" to find me some. (*Pause*) She must've gone in the back room and snapped a normal one in half.
Daniel (*standing*) Anyway. Bearing in mind everything ——
Lol (*pointing the buttybat at Daniel; sotto voce*) Sit down.

This is a significant moment. Daniel shoots a look at Adam, like a caged animal

Lol brandishes the club round, like a mafia boss toying with a machete

(*Pointing out Daniel to Esther*) See? (*He stands*) The first person ever who has ever wanted to leave one of your dinner parties. (*In a moment of genuine sympathy at the apocalyptic gravity of this he goes to Esther*) I'm sorry, love. I really am. Come here. (*And he holds her. He's still got the buttybat in one hand, though*) And you know why that is? Why this is all happening? It's happening — (*suddenly wielding the club at Daniel*) because someone started making up stories, didn't they Daniel?

Daniel freezes

Adam (*standing to defend Daniel*) Lol ——
Lol Is there such a thing as "Buttyball"?
Daniel I don't / know.
Lol *Is there?*
Adam *No!*
Lol *Inga Healey made up a story about this table.*
Adam *Yes.*
Lol *But it's worse than that, isn't it, Daniel?*
Adam *Yes.*
Daniel *Why?*
Adam *I don't know, I'm shouting 'cause he's shouting.*
Lol (*shouting*) She has made up a story about the table your grandfather rowed across the River Dee to visit your grandmother.

A slight pause. Adam and Daniel swallow

Adam ⎫
Daniel ⎭ (*together*) Yes.

Lol She has abused your family's history. She has taken it and — and — (*wielding the club*) done that.

Adam Well / that's ——

Lol (*brandishing the diddy club in the air*) Dwarfed it. She has done *that* to us. she has made us look like that. That — *bitch* ... (*He suddenly goes on the hunt for buttybats*)

Esther Where are you going?

Lol She never banked on us meeting, y'see, Esther. She clearly never banked on us ever meeting. But tonight, round this table, the English have met. There we go. (*He hands out the buttybats again during the following*)

Daniel I don't play.

Lol In case there's any trouble.

Adam ⎫
Bridget ⎭ (*together*)What?

Lol It's not much, but you'll be glad y've got it if an Alsatian comes at y'.

Esther Lol?

Lol They all have dogs, Germans. They're bloody cowardly bastards.

Esther You're not going to Inga's shop?

Lol exits to the kitchen to get his jacket

Bridget Dad, d'you not think a group of people marching angrily up a road with golf putters is going to look vaguely comical?

Lol We're not / marching ——

Bridget I mean why don't we just set fire to them and chant "Burn the witch"?

Lol We're not attacking her. It's self-defence. Christ, she might have security lights like ours. We won't know what's hit us till some bloke walks past on stilts.

Esther Why are you going to Inga's?

Lol My darling, to take the table back. Daniel, can you clear everything off your side?

Esther Don't.

Lol All the places.

Esther Don't touch those / places.

Lol *Clear the bloody plates.*

Everyone clears the table during the following, on reflex at the ferocity of this

Hey. (*To Esther*) You talk about friendship, about making friends out here. The art of friendship is knowing who to give it to and currently these guys — (*putting his arm round Daniel*) — I don't know about you, but I feel that having this thing in my house is making a mockery of them. Standing here with these planks where their family has lived and loved and — and died, standing here with this old rowing boat, I feel I'm being made a fool of.

Lol leaves a dramatic pause then exits into the yard, waving dramatically to activate the light

Esther watches him. And rises. She clears the remaining places and goes into the kitchen

Daniel, Adam and Bridget are left round the table. Pause

Daniel This is all my fault.
Bridget Dan, making the story up at the car boot sale was the right thing to do.
Daniel Yeah, with respect, and — and — and this is with respect, Bridget, with the *greatest* respect ——
Bridget Stop putting down crash mats.
Daniel You're a liar.
Adam (*sotto voce*) Dan?
Daniel She said it. You said that. And a liar telling me it's OK to lie is like an alcoholic, y'know? (*Gesturing*) "Have a drink, mate."

There's a clang on a milk churn outside

Lol (*off*) Arghhhybloodyy …
Bridget OK, but ——
Daniel No, not OK. It does (*gesturing to the room*) this, OK? You start doin' it, it causes this.

Lol enters, holding his leg

Lol Right. Stuff the light. We'll ——

The exterior light comes on

Oh, you little *sod*.
Bridget (*sotto voce*) You don't have to.
Lol Grab the back end.

Lol opens the other french window

Daniel (*sotto voce, sadly*) I do have to. It's my fault. (*He stands*)

Lol That lavender, y' see? That's what's at stake, here. That lavender is to the nose what Elgar is to the ears.

Lol picks up an end of the table. Daniel picks up the other end. They process out

Esther enters from the kitchen

Esther (*her head down*) I'm so sorry, Adam.

Esther picks up a lamp and follows the table out through the french windows, lamp held up. She exits

Bridget Good God. It's like a funeral cortège.

Bridget and Adam are left facing each other on two of the five chairs. Pause. The space is weird without the table

Adam You told Dan, then? About Vitor?
Bridget (*looking at Adam*) He asked not to be told.

Adam smiles. Then laughs

Adam Bless him.
Bridget He's not one of life's natural liars.
Adam (*picking at the label on his beer bottle*) Can't stand blood.
Bridget Maybe he needs toughening up.
Adam (*after a moment; smiling*) That was certainly me dad's opinion.
Bridget Maybe he was right.

Adam doesn't want to go there. There is a slight pause

Adam (*standing*) Come on.
Bridget (*waving her damson-gin-stained hands; wryly*) All get blood on our hands sometime.
Adam (*blowing a lamp out*) Not always of our own choosing.

Adam blows the candles in the salt miners' lamps out one by one during the following. Bridget watches him

Bridget 'Course it is.
Adam (*blowing a lamp out*) You're lying about Vitor but only so you have to go back to Portugal and avoid bloody —— (*waving*) "Zoom-Golf". It's

not — malicious, it's not bloody. It's just — you're like me. Y' got backed
into it.
Bridget (*frowning*) When?

Adam pauses and smiles

Adam (*nodding*) See if Big Dave got any rats.
Bridget What did you get backed into lying about, Mr Shellmedine?
Adam Keep telling him, if he wants to scare rats out he wants to start playing
Chris de Burgh.
Bridget I'll ask Daniel-I.

Adam looks at Bridget. She's waiting for an answer

Adam (*after a slight pause*) Daniel doesn't know.
Bridget (*playfully*) A lie you're keeping from your brother?
Adam (*blowing out a candle*) Sometimes the truth is so bad that people need
protection. (*He blows out another candle*)
Bridget By protection, you mean lies.
Adam (*sotto voce*) Stories.

Music plays: the first phrase of "Swingin' Safari". It stops dead

Pause. They share a wry smile

(*Pointing to the door*) Pudding?

Music plays: the second phrase of "Swingin' Safari". It stops dead

Bridget What's cooking?
Adam Sautéed witch.

Bridget stands

Bridget (*standing*) Yum.

Music plays: the full whack of "Swingin' Safari" crashes in

They throw back the doors and step out into the well-lit yard

Immediately the security light goes off

Black-out

ACT III
DESSERT

Inga's outhouse or shed (once a pigshed)

It has a dirty glass roof and contains what can only be described as a table graveyard; half-complete and damaged oak and pine tables lie all round the place. One is on its back with two legs missing at one end. There are two exits; one is a battered wooden shed door, leading to the outside world, the other a frosted-glass domestic door leading into the house

Music plays: "Swingin' Safari"

When the Act begins, moonlight streams through the dirty panes of the glass roof

The music stops. Silence. The wind whistles. An owl hoots. The headlights of a passing tractor strafe the room and then recede into the distance

The shadowy figure of Lol picks in through the wooden shed door

Lol My God.

Daniel enters behind Lol

Daniel Lol? I really don't think we should be going round the back of the shop.
Lol My-y God.
Daniel Lol?
Lol Have y' seen in here? It's like Crippen's basement.
Daniel Lol?
Lol Have y'seen these tables?
Daniel *Lol.*
Lol There's millions. She must stand on the road luring them in.
Daniel We're trespassing.
Lol "Come in, little table. I've got some lovely beeswax polish in my shed."
Daniel She might just not be in.
Lol Oh she's in. (*He looks in at the kitchen door*) She's in there all right. (*He turns like the hunters he's seen in films*) I can smell her. I can smell that bloody Germanic efficiency.

Esther (*off*) Lol?
Lol Esther! Esther come in here. Look at this.

Esther appears in the shed doorway followed by Adam and Bridget

Esther What are you doing?
Lol This is what it must've been like for them Russians stumbling on warehouses of stolen Nazi art.
Esther Precisely. They stumbled on it.
Lol Yes, well, stumbling sometimes involves trespassing, love. (*He picks his way round the room*) How d'y' think they discovered Tutankhamun's tomb? There wasn't a bloody lift.
Bridget You are illegally entering her / premises.
Lol Am I boll ... Look ... (*He points*) If she's not answering at the front, what d'you do? We can't help it if the back door's accessed through her — laboratory.
Bridget Whatever, she's / not going ——
Esther It's not a laboratory.
Bridget She's not coming out, so / let's ——
Lol Obviously she's not going to come out. Obviously she's not going to come out. (*Pause*) We'll have to lure her out.
Bridget I'm sorry?
Lol (*gesturing*) Lads?
Esther What d'you mean, lure?
Lol I mean lure.
Esther How?
Lol With a trap. How does one normally lure?
Esther I don't know. I've never lured.
Lol Well then.
Esther I didn't intend to spend tonight luring. I thought by eleven-seventeen we'd be on coffee and mints.
Lol Yes an' who've you got to thank for that? (*Pointing*) Doctor bloody Frankentable.
Esther Stop calling her that.
Lol Where d'y drop the table?
Daniel Er ——
Adam In the car park.
Lol She'll see it! It can't stay there. We've gotta get it out of view or she'll smell a rat. Come on.
Bridget God Almighty. It's like *The Dirty Dozen*.
Lol That's ... (*Pointing*) Yes. Exactly what it's like. Come on.

Lol ushers Daniel and Adam out

Mother and daughter are alone in the pigshed

Esther I thought we'd be on coffee and mints. (*Pause*) In Foxhill Grove
we'd've been on coffee and mints.

There is a pause

Bridget Yeah. Well, it's not Foxhill Grove any more, is it?

There is a pause. We hear sounds of the night

Esther What's he like?

Bridget looks at her mum

Vitor?

This isn't what Bridget expected. She sobers slightly

What do his family do?

Bridget looks at Esther

His mother. Does she work? What's her name?
Bridget Er ... b-er ... Marietta.

Pause

Esther It's sometimes harder, Bridget. In other countries. For women. You
mustn't let him hold you back. (*She looks up*) You must promise me that.
If you feel that starting to happen, you come home.
Bridget Like it doesn't happen round here.

*Pause. Bridget looks at her mum. In one second she's probably closer to her
than she's been in her life. Esther looks out. The point is taken*

Esther (*with a wry smile*) Don't worry about me, love. I used to deliver
catalogues.

Bridget looks at her questioningly

When your dad's works got taken over. And we'd just bought the
bungalow. (*She smiles wryly at the memory*) He always thought it was a bit

off, y'r dad, seeing it was a German company who took over and he drank
Riesling and we went on a Rhine cruise for our honeymoon. I think he'd
thought that'd sort of secure him his job. But er ... (*Obviously it didn't*) Any
road. His answer was to start drinking industrial amounts of Riesling,
which is — fine. Some people aren't fighters. Your dad's not, love, I have
to warn y'. Your dad's one of them people who does road rage by sticking
the "Vs" up soon as he's dead sure the other driver's stayin' on the
motorway and he's going off up the sliproad.

Bridget What catalogues?

Esther The same ones me mum used to do. Round Runcorn. And I felt
maybe this is what happens, Bridget. We slip. Gradually we all slip back
where we belong. (*She pauses slightly*) But I didn't, y'see. Even as a kid,
sitting in that Hillman Imp on the Linfield Estate, watching mum collect
bloody fivers for bloody toasted sandwich makers ... (*She pauses slightly.
The memory is still chilling. She shakes her head*) Round here. Is where I
belong. I'm not being held back anywhere, sweetheart. I'm in Almanley.

Lol stomps back in

Lol Right. Here we go.

Daniel follows Lol on

Daniel Lol. It's going to get ruined.

Lol Everyone ready?

Daniel You can't just stand it / in ——

Lol OK now I want you to just talk like normal-talking.

Daniel — in the field. / It's ——

Lol Like we're on a safari party. Sort of jovially. Sort of "Really?" "Aha!"
"*Really?*"

Adam Lol it's not safe for / the ——

Lol Look, it can take standing in a field a couple of minutes. Good God,
someone's rowed across the River Dee on those timbers (*He knocks on the
kitchen door*) Inga love? We're here for our pudding. (*Gesturing to the
others encouragingly*) Come on. "Hahaha, hmm, oo really?" (*Through the
door*) We sort of lost you after the hors d'oeuvres.

Daniel Lol, we ——

Lol *Shhhh-t.*

A light comes on behind the kitchen door. Lol joyously does a thumbs-up

(*Through the door, loudly*) Yes, I think you probably didn't understand the
whole ... You know. The concept, love. You were supposed to come to
ours for the main course.

Inga appears in silhouette behind the frosted glass of the door

Lol does a football gesture of triumph

Yeah? Then we all come to yours for pudding.
Inga Get out.

Pause

Lol Have y' done a pudding?
Esther Lol ——

Lol silences Esther with a vicious air-swipe

Lol We're all here, love.
Inga You've made your point with your Tollycurney rubbish.

Lol turns, amazed, to the lads

Lol She thinks you made it up. Classic. *She* does it, she thinks everyone else
    does it.
Bridget (*sotto voce*) Dad ——
Lol (*sotto voce*) Sorry, love. These lads' ancestors *ate* Tollycurney.
Inga There is no such thing as Tollycurney.

Lol gestures "I don't believe it" to those this side of the door

Lol Tell y', y'wanna come out and talk to these lads, love. They grew up in
    Cheshire.
Inga So did I.
Lol Yeah well not properly, love. With respect, their family tree is solid
    birch, not half Bavarian spruce.
Bridget *Dad.*
Lol (*sotto voce*) She can take a joke.

Inga disappears from behind the door and the light goes out

Bridget She's gone in.
Lol She ... Eh? (*He turns to look at the door*)
Bridget Well done.
Lol See? Humour, y' see? It's like showing crosswords to fish.
Adam Eh?
Lol (*knocking on the door*) Tell a German a joke, it's like blowing up a bull's
    nostrils. Stops 'em dead.

Esther Let's just go. You've made your point.

Lol (*suddenly very grandly*) How many more have to suffer?

Bridget (*closing her eyes*) Oh for fff ...

Lol How many more innocents are going to be sold snapped-off putters? How many — I mean ... (*Shouting at the door and knocking*) This table here, Inga. (*He points to the one that's on its back with two legs missing at one end*) Are you going to replace the two missing legs or just say it was customary for farmers to sit with one end on their laps?

Adam (*making to leave*) Maybe we / should ——

Lol (*loudly*) I didn't buy a table, Inga. I bought a Buttyball table. (*He pauses, then heads out. For Adam and Daniel's benefit*) Two and a half we paid for that table.

Lol exits

(*Off*) An' we're getting it back.

Daniel (*suddenly, from nowhere, to no-one in particular*) There's no such thing as Tollycurney.

Adam and Bridget exchange a quick look

Adam (*suddenly*) Come on, let's help him.

Daniel I'm sorry.

Adam (*taking Daniel's arm*) Get the table back in here.

Esther What?

Adam Dan. He's going to need a hand.

Daniel (*not moving*) We didn't have time to make a proper starter because we had to go out and buy a table, because she'd bought our table, 'cause we had to sell something, and that's why we wanted this meal, because ——

Adam Mneeeek.

Daniel No. I've had it.

A slight pause hangs in the air

We were after a contract mowing your paddock. We thought eighty quid a month, bloody hell ... (*To Adam*) "That'd keep us going. That'd change everything". Well, it won't. It won't change anything. It'd just make shit better. It'd just do what we do to that sodding landfill. Spray a bit of lavender on for a bit.

Bridget Spray what?

Daniel (*turning*) Oh aye. That's what we do. We've a contract with the Dutch firm who manage the landfill to mow the grass on that tip then pull tankers full of scented water over it 'cause people round here complained about the smell.

There is a slight pause. Adam rubs his eyes in a "game's up" kind of way

Adam Mmmmph.
Daniel And I tell y', y' drive over that hill, and the sun's out and the radio's
on in the tractor cab, and you're telling yourself, "This is all right. This is
almost like farming."

There is a slight pause

Whereas in fact we're rolling deodorant on to the shirt armpit of North
Cheshire.

Pause, in which only the ironic sound of an approaching tractor is audible

Esther There's no such thing as Tollycurney?

The others look at her

I was going to serve people that.
Bridget You still can.
Esther Not if it's not Tollycurney. If it's not Tollycurney it's just bacon and
cold cheese.

Pause. Esther looks down

I thought — when you told me about it, I thought y'd been having such a
good chat with Daniel in that pantry. I thought y'd really been getting on.
Bridget Well we … We were. We had. Hadn't we? (*She looks at Daniel*)

Pause. Esther looks at Bridget

Esther (*quietly, honestly*) She's smashing, in't she?

*Suddenly a wooden missile comes crashing through the glass roof. Everyone
bolts for cover. It's followed by a dustfall of wood shavings and chips. The
tractor sound stops*

*There is a pause. Adam sticks his head above the parapet first. He inspects
the shavings, the missile … The others emerge like frightened cavemen —
and look up at the new hole in the glass which casts its shape on the bothy floor*

Lol rushes in, blood all over his face

Oh my God. Oh my God.

There's a slightly surreal pause. Lol, panting, suddenly picks up the wooden missile

Adam What's happened?
Lol (*after a slight pause; bellowing*) Inga?
Esther *Lol*?
Bridget Dad! What's / that?
Lol (*wielding the missile*) That? That is our kitchen table. That is our kitchen table after it's been run over by a combine harvester.
Adam (*to Daniel*) Oh my God. Big Dave.
Lol (*staggering slightly*) There's a bloke out there with two guns an' a combine harvester that's playing rap music.

The kitchen door is thrown open and Inga lurches in with two huge pairs of antique sheep-shears, easily eighteen inches long, like Edward Scissorhands

Inga *Get out.*
Lol (*heading out through the shed door at speed*) Jesus God. (*He stops in the yard beyond the door*)
Esther *Oh my God.*
Adam Bloody hell.
Bridget Inga!
Adam Inga, put them down. Come on.
Inga *Get out of my bothy.*
Lol What?
Daniel Shed.
Esther Shant.
Lol What?
Adam Look all it is, Inga / is ——
Daniel Lol just wants a refund.
Lol (*pointing through the doorway*) Yes, *refund.*
Adam Give me the shears, Inga.
Bridget We're going.
Lol We're not.
Esther Inga, sweetheart / we ——
Lol We are not going anywhere.
Daniel Lol, just ——
Lol (*pointing*) We're going to let it be known round Almanley that Inga Healey makes up history to suit her antiques. (*Sensing a trump card*) That's where we're going.
Inga Well, then, maybe I should let it be known round Almanley that the Voyseys have a conservatory.

Pause

Esther Why?

Inga lowers the weapon, now superseded

(*Turning to Lol with a dinner-party smile*) Lol?
Inga Up their long lane. Conveniently hidden. Maybe I should do that.
Esther Why, what would ——? Conservatories, what's ——?

Inga turns to go with her shears

It's the Henley. What's the problem with the Henley? Aren't you allowed
Henleys?
Lol 'Course we're not, love. What are you thinking about? We can't build
a conservatory on our own barn.

Inga turns

Our own property. God, what are / you ——
Inga Your property is in the green belt, Mr Voysey. Your land is my
countryside.

Inga exits into the house

Pause. The house light goes off. Pause

Lol (*calling after Inga*) And you expect me to believe anything from the
mouth that came up with Buttyball? (*Turning to Adam*) That's bollocks,
isn't it? You're allowed conservatories.
Esther Adam?
Lol It's a God-given right. That's like saying you're not allowed feet.
Esther (*to Adam*) Can you have conservatories?
Daniel Well it's ... (*He winces and shrugs*) I ——
Lol What?
Daniel (*jumping slightly*) Aargh.
Adam Dad wanted to make the butty into / a ——
Bridget Bothy.
Adam Bothy into a house when we started ... When money started getting
tight, but he ——

Pause. A heavy pall is descending

Daniel The Parish Council said if the countryside lost too many run-down
sheds it wouldn't look like the countryside.

Pause. Everyone looks back at Lol

Lol No way. No way is she gonna win this. (*He points at the kitchen door*) No way.

Lol exits through the shed door, slightly dramatically

Adam He won't do anything, Esther.

A beat

Let's face it, Lol ain't the kind of guy to take on someone who might put up a fight.

Esther (*standing; gently*) No, love. (*She moves to the door. Smiling, almost sadly*) I know he isn't.

Esther exits after Lol

The three remaining sit still amongst the table graveyard for a few beats. Bridget frowns a smile at Adam

Adam (*seeing Bridget's look; sotto voce*) He's just very familiar.

A look passes from Adam to Daniel

Bridget Your dad?
Adam Slightly less — physical ——
Daniel (*sotto voce*) Don't.

Pause

Bridget What?

Pause. Daniel eyes Adam

Like what?

Adam eyes say to Daniel, "You gonna answer this?"

Daniel Don't.
Adam Why d'y think I ended up having to hide the bloody golf club in the shed?
Bridget (*sotto voce*) No. (*She looks to Daniel for verification*)

Adam (*to Daniel*) Can I at this point remind you of that massive stand you made about not lying.

Daniel Look, his farm had collapsed, OK? He'd lost the Sparkbrook herd, Bridget, and I cannot tell y' — the "Sparkbrook herd", four generations, famous across the county and pfffrt: compulsory purchase order. "Your land's gonna be a tip, mate. Sorry." And there's something happens, something — when a man loses the one thing that defines him ...

Bridget It makes it all right for him to lay into his kids?

Daniel stops dead. He looks to Adam who looks down

Dunno who's worst. The guy who does it — or the victim who makes excuses for it. Dunno who's weakest.

A pause hangs

Daniel (*stung*) And so what's "weak", Bridget? In fact? Exactly? In your ... Your — fantastic summing-up / of ——?

Bridget Someone who needs protection? (*She shrugs. She playfully, but dead seriously, turns the focus to Adam*) But there again ... Y'know. Whose fault's *that*? The guy who needs protection, or the guy who keeps him protected without him knowing? (*She does an "eyes-up" to Adam*)

Daniel follows Bridget's gaze, unsure of the territory suddenly

Daniel The thing is, Bridget, with respect, you don't know the full story OK? And yeah, OK, maybe I wouldn't make allowances if me dad hadn't regretted so much, OK, hadn't in the end come to regret what he did to me *so* much that *he bloody shot himself. OK?* (*He points to Adam*) *Did he tell you that? That's why he did it. That's why Dad bloody shot himself.*

Adam (*sotto voce*) He didn't.

Pause. Adam looks down

(*Quietly, rubbing his eyes*) He didn't. (*Looking up at Dan finally*) I'm sorry, Dan. I'd love him to 've committed suicide out of guilt, but he just ... He wouldn't. (*He pauses*) You should've thought, really, mate. Six shots. (*He puts a finger through one of the holes*) You don't put six holes in a table trying to commit suicide. Even if you're moving about a bit to make it more challenging for yourself.

Daniel (*sotto voce*) Oh no.

Adam My intention — Dan, I went in that kitchen, honest to God, all I was intending to say was that if he laid into you again we were out. Gone. He'd be on his own in his pissbowl of a farm. That is all I was planning on saying.

Daniel (*sotto voce*) No no no / no ——
Adam But when I walked in ——
Daniel (*deathly*) Don't want to hear this.
Adam — when I walked into that kitchen ——
Daniel *I don't want* ——
Adam — there was this rat.

Pause

Bridget I'm sorry?
Adam This — (*gesturing the size*) quite big rat that'd come in off the landfill,
an' it was like running round the skirting boards. And Dad was on the table,
in his pyjamas, with a bottle of vodka, loading up the shotgun. And he sees
me and he goes, "Right, watch and learn." And he starts trying to shoot this
rat, right? And the first shot misses by miles, (*gesturing*) goes flying out
down the yard, but it scares the crap out of this rat, right, who now starts
pegging it in all directions over the floor with Dad shouting "Stay still you
little bastard." Until finally it heads under the table, which makes Dad freak
'cause he hates rats, so he starts firing at the rat through the table, round after
bloody round, until finally, completely by chance, he hits the rat an' kills
it. At which point he shouts "Hahargh! Dirty Harry!", swings the gun round
his middle finger and accidentally shoots himself through the jaw.

Pause

(*Quietly, gesturing loosely…*) He fell sort of odd. Sort of — back on his
knees like a limbo dancer. Position y' only see when people are having a
great time an' there's laughing an' that. Steel drums. Only it was just him
an' me. An' no noise. Until the sound of blood hitting the lino.

Pause

(*Looking up at Dan again*) I'd love him to've apologized, mate. More than
anything I'd've loved that. But his last words were "Hahargh. Dirty
Harry."

Lol strides in, muddy-trousered with a muddy table leg

Lol Right, we're claiming that two-legged table.

They turn

(*Brandishing the table leg*) Two of our legs were salvage-able. Your
mother's … (*Looking round*) She was heading back here with the other
one.

Inga (*off*) *Put it down!*

They all turn

  (*Off*) *Please! Esther!*
Bridget (*sotto voce*) Esther?
Inga (*off*) *Put it down.*
Bridget Oh fff ——

The kitchen door bangs open and Inga flies out

Inga *Stop her!*
Bridget Whoa.
Inga (*pointing behind her*) *She smashed the door with a table leg.* (*Pointing*)
  Tell her to put it down!

  *Esther enters from the kitchen carrying a tray of crockery. Everything
  tinkles*

Esther (*"smiling", calm*) Oh, I'll put it down, Inga. I'll put the tray down.
  The only question is — from what height?
Adam What's the / matter?
Daniel What is it?
Esther What is it? It's a tea service, boys. Belonging to the last surviving
  navvy to work on the Manchester Ship Canal.

Pause

  Now. Let's talk about my conservatory.

Everyone looks at Inga

Inga If you think I'm going to succumb to / a ——

Esther drops a plate to the floor

  No!
Lol Esther?
Adam (*sotto voce to Inga*) Sorry to ask, but is it *really* the last surviving / nav
  ——?
Inga *Yes.*
Adam Right, just checking / the ——
Daniel Listen / let's ——
Lol Esther / just ——

Esther *Shut up.*

Everyone takes a step back

Let's hear what you're going to say, here in your falling-down shed: why
I am not allowed the most beautiful conservatory in the brochure. I want
to know exactly, in detail, in — in — in detail, what is not beautiful about
the Henley.

Inga It's not about beauty. It's about being in keeping / with ——

Esther And this is?

Inga What?

Esther We're allowed shitty things that are falling down, are we? I'm
allowed a sh-hitty — shant?

Bridget (*half in alarm, half in admiration*) Mum?

Inga I'm not prepared to stand here and ...

Esther raises a sideplate

No-o! They're not my rules. They're here to protect the countryside.

Esther Yes. Yes. (*Bitterly*) From me. Aren't they, Inga? Not for me. *From
me.*

Adam Esther ——

Inga It's not in keeping. Barns did not have conservatories.

Esther (*finally losing it*) *Barns didn't have people living in them either!*

Lol Steady-y ——

Esther (*almost shaking*) She is not having my conservatory.

Adam Give me the / tray.

Daniel Give him the tray, Esther.

*Adam takes hold of the tray handles. Finally, she releases her hold on the
tray. Everyone breathes out slightly*

Lol Thank you.

*Adam moves to take the tray to safety. Esther snatches up the covered cake
dish*

Inga *No-o!*

Esther Oh-ho-ho-hoh 'cause this is the jewel, isn't it, Inga? I know. You said.
The cake dish is worth six hundred pounds on its own, isn't it? (*A slight
pause*) Or was that only to me? Was that only to me because (*she reacts
to the first prick of tears*) — this stupid bantam you were getting pally with
thought ... (*the following hits her as she says it. It pricks her eyes*) who
really thought ... (*She cries*)

Everyone's a bit awkward, because yes, she's really crying. Finally ...

Inga Look inside.

Esther gently applies the tear-brakes

Look inside it.

Esther lowers the cake dish. She looks at it. Everyone's interested now. Gingerly Esther makes to remove the china lid

Lol (*as though it might be primed*) Careful.

So, so, gently with a single "chink" of fine porcelain, the lid is removed. Inside the dish sits a rather rudimentary cake

Inga That's the first cake I've made in twenty years.
Lol (*pointing*) She's off again! She ... Bloody hell, she can't help it!
Adam Lol ——
Lol Was it made using the only eggs that survived the crash of the Hindenburg?
Inga (*to Esther*) You started coming in, you see. After you bought the table. You started coming in and — and — and chatting and I thought "Well, what do I do? Do I risk ——? Do I ... ? Should I tell her there's no such thing as Buttyball?"

Pause

(*Loosely gesturing towards the lads*) Which is what you've obviously found out. Which is obviously the only reason you invited me. (*Swallowing*) It's been — it was hard bec ... (*Quietly*) I liked Esther.
Lol Oh, I bet, love. I bet you liked Esther. (*He moves round the room in typical Lol fashion*) Poor old gullible Esther. Poor stupid old trusting Esther. Poor old Esther who swallowed your story of Buttyball hook, line and sinker.
Daniel Whereas of course rapier-minded Lol saw straight through it.

Daniel suddenly stands and takes command of the cake dish. He just as suddenly fronts Lol off

Rapier-brain Lol knew immediately there wasn't such thing as "Buttyball".
Lol Eh? (*He looks at Esther*)

Adam looks at Bridget

Daniel No, he fell for it. You want to know why he fell for it? Because it is bloody *fantastic*. (*He puts the cake dish down in safety*) As stories go ... "Rural golf"? "On a table"? That is just so completely, completely brilliant it makes me want to throw my hands in the air and say, "Yes, Inga, yes, that actually, that *is* worth two and a half thousand pounds a table."

Lol How can you say that, when your grandad / sat ——

Daniel Particularly compared to the story I made up about me grandad rowing it across the bloody River Dee.

Pause. Everyone looks at everyone else

Sorry, Lol. I can't be pissed off with someone committing a crime, when all they've done is commit it better than I did.

Lol This table — that your ancestors ate Tollycurney off, wasn't rowed / across —— ?

Bridget There isn't / such ——

Adam There's no / such ——

Esther There's no such thing as Tollycurney, Lol.

Lol What?

Esther She made / that ——

Bridget I made that up.

Pause

Lol Christ almighty.

Inga (*looking down*) Things aren't good in antiques. "Genuine" isn't enough. It's got to be genuine *and* some. It's got to have a history.

Lol *Yeah, but a real one, eh? A real one, that's / the* ——

Daniel OK, Lol. Here we go. Welcome to Rural Cheshire Antiques. You want a table? Certainly, sir. How about this one? A fine six-by-three foot table, solid oak, taken from the home of a bitter alcoholic who physically abused his kids and died unrepentant, trying to shoot a rat whilst in his pyjamas. How much is that worth eh, Lol? How much would you pay for that bit of Cheshire history?

Pause

My dad's life was worth fuck all, Lol. I'd stick with Buttyball.

Lol looks at Daniel with some new regard. As does everyone. Lol is genuinely quietened by Daniel's speech, and the gravity of the story

Lol Right. I didn't know. (*Pause*) Right. (*His tone for the first time is* *sympathetic*) Prob'ly best gone under a combine harvester then, eh? (*He sends a sort of sympathetic smile across to Daniel. Waving loosely*) Organic end.

Pause

Daniel (*sotto voce, nodding*) Good name for your barn.

Lol smiles in spite of himself

Inga Take a table. (*She exhaustedly just waves a hand*)

Pause

Esther D'you mean that?
Inga (*not looking up*) No point having y'r — conservatory without a table.

Everyone sort of looks at each other

Lol Right. Well that's very … (*He nods*)

There is an awkward pause

Esther Any partic / ular ——?
Inga (*waving*) They're all the same. They're all just tables. I don't have any more buttyballs.
Lol No. Well. Y' wouldn't.

Lol and Esther stand and look around

(*Sotto voce*) That one looks … (*He gestures "What do you think of this one?" at a table, to Esther*)

Esther complies, silently

D'you want to, er …?

Lol and Esther up-end one if the tables and arrange themselves at either end of one of it. This is all reminiscent of the removal of a corpse

Bridget makes to leave

Adam Hope things work out with Vitor.

Bridget stops a second

Hope he turns out to be strong for you.

We expect a tart riposte from Bridget but we don't get one. She turns and makes to leave — but then the second jab comes

By which of course I mean "Not weak."

Bridget stops again

(*Playfully, but dead seriously*) By which I mean you don't have to spend the rest of your life protecting him.

A moment

Esther (*an instruction to go*) Bridget?

Bridget exits

Lol Right.
Esther Right.
Lol Right.

But there's nothing really to say

Esther Well. (*Pause*) Thanks for coming, everyone.

They all look at her

Lol heads out of the shed door. Esther, at the other end of the table, follows. They exit

The two lads and Inga remain in silence

Daniel (*holding his hand out to Inga but not looking at her*) Daniel, by the way.

Inga looks at him then shakes his hand somewhat perfunctorily

Inga Inga.

Somewhere outside there's a single gunshot

What's that?

Adam Sounds like he got one.

There are more gunshots in rapid succession

Inga Who?
Daniel Big Dave.
Adam It's just a friend of ours. Farmer. Goes out at night shooting rats.
Bridget (*off*) Ladies and gentlemen.

Bridget saunters in with two large field guns

I'm afraid I have to report a death.

Esther staggers, gasping, to the shed door. Her dress has been caught, and contributes, post-teatray-frenzy, to an increasingly wild-woman appearance

Adam ⎱
Daniel ⎰ (*together*) *Argh!*
Esther (*her eyes begging for answers*) Why?
Bridget (*to Esther*) Bring him in. Don't leave him on the road. People are gonna notice.
Inga (*in a deathly whisper*) What have you done?
Bridget Now, Daniel? To get away with this, I'm going to have to ask you to lie, OK? Which I know you don't like doing, but that's what it's gonna take. (*Calling*) Come on, come on, come on. In we come.

Lol walks in, slightly zombified, dragging the table. He too looks ravaged, bloodied, his hair awry ...

Lol (*eyes wide*) She shot the table.
Bridget Keep coming. In the middle.

Lol and Esther carry the table to the middle of the room

Adam What?
Bridget (*directing the table down*) That's the way. OK. Back off a bit.

Lol backs off

Lol (*slightly on auto-redial*) She shot the / table ——
Bridget No, no, no. (*Holding a finger up*) Shhh. *I* didn't shoot this table. (*Leaning in*) This table was shot by an old man. One hundred and fifty years ago. (*Looking round*) Because if it *was* ... (*turning*) Buttyball exists.

Pause. They all look at the table in the middle of the room

And if Buttyball exists, (*to Esther*) you've got a table with a rural history. (*To Inga*) And you ... (*She looks round at the graveyard of tables*)

Everyone follows her gaze, and looks round too

(*As to children*) Who *knows* how many Buttyball tables there were in Cheshire.

They look round at what now feels like Tutankhamun's tomb

Who knows how much sheer — *joy* lies in this room for the antique-buying public? And should any of them say they've never heard of "Buttyball", (*gesturing*) up the Ridgeway you point them, up to the gates of Sparkbrooke farm. Where once — (*gesturing*) one Autumn evening, slate grey sky, ruddy-cheeked from the mowing, old Jacob Shellmedine came home, downed a mug of damson gin and thought, "Bugger me. What I really fancy now is a game of golf." (*She looks round*) I know you can't put a price on two brothers' family history, Inga. But how about a cut of four hundred quid for every table sold?

Bridget picks up a buttybat

Plus of course ten per cent for the businesswoman who thought of it.

Lol looks at his daughter with rising admiration. Probably because it's the first time in fifteen years they've been talking the same language

Ha haaa-a! (*She does a little drum roll on the table*) Y'see the person who's died tonight is Vitor. Because he only existed to stop me having to run a golf shop! (*She turns to Adam and puts her arms out in a sort of "There, I've done it too" kind of way*)

Adam smiles, and does a little silent clap

So! Do we all, in this bothy gathered here tonight, solemnly swear that Buttyball was a game played by hitting *that* ball, with *that* bat, into *that* hole to score a point?
Daniel (*sotto voce*) No.

Everyone looks at Daniel

I'm sorry. I can't have Dad's family history screwed up like this. (*He pauses*) See, the *central* ones were worth a point. The ones near the edge were *three*.

Music: the first phrase of 'Swingin' Safari'. It stops dead

Inga (*sotto voce; looking round*) Y-yessss.
Daniel (*sotto voce, nodding*) More difficult.
Inga (*nodding*) The ones on the edge.

Pause

Esther (*moving on to the quarry*) In fact, the one at the *back* ...

Music plays: the second phrase of "Swingin' Safari". It stops dead

Inga Five.
Daniel That was worth / five.
Esther Five points.

Inga moves in on the prey

Daniel In fact, as I remember, I used to be family champion.

Adam moves in on the quarry

Adam Well then.

Music plays: the third phrase of "Swingin' Safari". It stops dead

Adam grimly rolls up his sleeves

Daniel I think history might need some avenging.
Lol (*passing Adam a club like a scalpel*) One buttybat.
Daniel Buttybat. It's all coming back to me now.
Inga Yes-s. (*A slight pause*) Anyone fancy some pudding?

Music plays: the insistent bound of "Swingin' Safari" at full volume

Everyone plays the ancient rural game of Buttyball and eat Inga's cake, chattering

The Lights gradually fade to Black-out

FURNITURE AND PROPERTY LIST

ACT I

Off stage: MFI flatpack containing: sheet of instructions, parts of a circular table, plastic bag of screws and nails (**Adam** and **Daniel**)
Ashtray, beanbag, fold-out director's chair (**Adam**)
Heel from Esther's shoe (**Lol**)
Old office swivel chair, fold-out director's chair (**Adam**)
Bottle of wine, odd selection of glasses including Coke-branded glass, Silver Jubilee glass, Road Runner glass (**Daniel**)
Battered old electric fire with fake log effect (practical), extension cable (**Daniel**)
Tiny stool, tiny bowl of crisps (**Adam**)
Crisps (**Bridget**)
Golf club (**Lol**)
Plates (**Daniel**)
Plate of bacon and cheese (**Bridget**)

Personal: **Bridget**: packet of cigarettes, lighter
Daniel: bloodied bandage

ACT II

On stage: 6ft by 3ft table with six bulletholes. *On it*: red gingham tablecloth, six place settings, plates etc.
Six dining chairs

Off stage: Four salt miners' lamps with lighted candles in them (any hurricane-style lamp will suffice) (**Esther**)
Two bottles of beer (**Bridget**)
Kitchen roll (**Esther**)
Bottle of beer (**Bridget**)
White ball the size of a large marble, four small putters (**Lol**)
Hawaiian Chicken in a dish (**Esther**)
Large green milk churn (**Lol**)
Earthenware jug full of damson gin (**Bridget**)

ACT III

On stage: Several half-complete and damaged oak and pine tables; one on its
              back with two legs missing

Off stage: Wooden missile — shard of Act II table with bullet holes — wood
              shavings and chips (**Stage Management**)
              Antique sheep-shears (**Inga**)
              Muddy table leg (**Lol**)
              Tray of crockery including cake dish with rudimentary-looking cake
              in it (**Esther**)
              Two large field guns (**Bridget**)

LIGHTING PLOT

Practical fittings required: ACT I: glowing electric heater, fluorescent strip light
Three interiors

ACT I

To open: General interior lighting with strip light

Cue 1	**Daniel** plugs in electric fire	(Page 9)
	Bring up additional log flicker effect	
Cue 2	**Adam** and **Daniel** exit	(Page 29)
	Black-out	

ACT II

To open: Moonlight

Cue 3	**Esther** enters; pause	(Page 30)
	Snap on floodlight outside conservatory	
Cue 4	**Esther** turns on the overhead lights	(Page 30)
	Snap on overhead lights	
Cue 5	**Esther** exits into the kitchen	(Page 30)
	Snap on light in kitchen	
Cue 6	**Esther** enters carrying a salt miners' lamp	(Page 31)
	Bring up covering spot on candle	
Cue 7	**Lol**: "… as John F. Kennedy."	(Page 31)
	Snap off floodlight. Flicker spot on salt miners' lamp	
Cue 8	**Esther** enters with two more lamps	(Page 31)
	Bring up covering spot on candles	
Cue 9	**Esther** enters with another lamp	(Page 32)
	Bring up covering spot on candle	
Cue 10	**Esther** dims the overhead lights	(Page 40)
	Dim overhead lights; pause; snap up floodlight	

| *Cue* 11 | **Esther**: " Playing Buttyball." | (Page 41) |
| | *Snap off floodlight* | |

| *Cue* 12 | **Esther**: " ... down the salt mines." Pause | (Page 46) |
| | *Snap on floodlight; pause; snap off floodlight* | |

| *Cue* 13 | **Lol**: "Right. Stuff the light. We'll ——" | (Page 49) |
| | *Snap on floodlight* | |

| *Cue* 14 | **Esther** exits with the lamp | (Page 50) |
| | *Cut covering spot on lamp* | |

| *Cue* 15 | **Adam**: "Come on." | (Page 50) |
| | *Cut covering spots on lamps as* **Adam** *blows out the candles* | |

| *Cue* 16 | **Bridget** and **Adam** step out into the yard | (Page 51) |
| | *Snap off floodlight; then black-out* | |

ACT III

To open: Moonlight

| *Cue* 17 | When ready | (Page 52) |
| | *Headlights of passing tractor strafe the room* | |

| *Cue* 18 | **Lol**: *"Shhhh-t."* | (Page 55) |
| | *Bring up light behind glass door* | |

| *Cue* 19 | **Inga** disappears from behind the door | (Page 56) |
| | *Cut light behind glass door* | |

| *Cue* 20 | The door is thrown open | (Page 59) |
| | *Bring up light beyond door* | |

| *Cue* 21 | **Inga** exits into the house. Pause | (Page 60) |
| | *Cut light behind glass door* | |

| *Cue* 22 | **Inga**: "Put it down!" They all turn | (Page 64) |
| | *Bring up light behind glass door* | |

| *Cue* 23 | Everyone plays the game and chatters | (Page 72) |
| | *Gradually fade to black-out* | |

EFFECTS PLOT

ACT I

Cue 1   **Adam**: " ... or make the table?"   (Page 1)
Doorbell

Cue 2   **Adam**: " '... and fittings.'"   (Page 2)
Doorbell

Cue 3   **Daniel**: "OK, now even on *Ready, Steady, Cook* ..."   (Page 3)
Doorbell

Cue 4   **Adam**: "Nn-n-no."   (Page 5)
Loud clang

Cue 5   **Bridget**: "... phenomenally embarrassing." Pause   (Page 15)
Doorbell

Cue 6   **Esther**: "I presumed —— "   (Page 15)
Doorbell

Cue 7   **Adam**: "I was there. You weren't."   (Page 28)
Toilet flushes

Cue 8   **Adam** turns to **Daniel**   (Page 29)
Music: "Swingin' Safari" by The Bert Kaempfert Orchestra

ACT II

Cue 9   As ACT II begins   (Page 30)
Music: "Swingin' Safari"

Cue 10   **Esther** hobbles in   (Page 30)
Cut "Swingin' Safari"

Cue 11   Floodlight suddenly goes off   (Page 41)
Clang

Cue 12   **Daniel**: "'Have a drink, mate.'"   (Page 49)
Clang

Cue 13   **Adam**: "Stories."   (Page 51)
Music: first phrase of "Swingin' Safari" ; cut

ACT III